beyond oatmeal

101 breakfast recipes

ISBN: 978-159955-018-3

Published by CFI, an imprint of Cedar Fort, Inc., 2373 W. 700 S., Springville, UT, 84663
Distributed by Cedar Fort, Inc. www.cedarfort.com

LIBRARY OF CONGRESS CATALOGING-IN-PUBLICATION DATA

Duda, Carlene, 1962-
    Beyond Oatmeal: 101 breakfast recipes / Carlene Duda.
        p. cm.
    ISBN 978-1-59955-018-3
    1. Breakfasts. I. Title. II. Title: One hundred one breakfast recipes.

    TX733.D84 2007
    641.5'2--dc22

2006101936

Cover and page design by Nicole Williams
Edited by Annaliese B. Cox
Cover design © 2007 by Lyle Mortimer

Printed in China

10 9 8 7 6 5 4 3 2 1

Printed on acid-free paper

beyond oatmeal

101 breakfast recipes

Carlene Duda

CFI
Springville, Utah

"Eat your oatmeal; it will put hair on your chest!"

That's what my dad would always say. Like that's really going to convince kids to eat their breakfast!

Good food, good people, and good times go hand in hand. Having worked several years in the catering and restaurant business, I've noticed that people flock to where the food is. Food just attracts people. And why not? It's a great excuse to gather together and share stories. What better way is there to share our time, means, and skills with others than over a great meal. This cookbook is designed to help you share some good food with good friends—and have a fun time doing it.

contents

Breakfast Memories

● How It All Started

Is there more to breakfast than just oatmeal? Growing up I thought everyone ate oatmeal for breakfast because it was a morning food staple in my family. As a kid, I detested oatmeal so much that I would sit staring at the unappetizing form in my bowl, hoping if I sat at the table long enough, it would go away or eventually evaporate. Of course, it never did. The longer I sat and looked at the bowl of oatmeal, the more it seemed to augment into a mountain of thick, lumpy glue surrounded by a moat of cold milk. I had to eat it; leaving it on the table was *not* an option. And yet, the more I struggled to choke it down, the more it seemed to expand. Eventually Mom tried to coax all of us into trying it with milk, brown sugar, and even raisins. She tried everything she could think of to coerce us into eating the dreaded breakfast cereal. It is because of these memories, engraved in my mind forever, that I have sought to find out if there is more to breakfast than just oatmeal. And this cookbook is the answer.

● Breakfast at Grandma's

Breakfast at Grandma's was my "Breakfast at Tiffany's." It never consisted of oatmeal, and my twin sister and I welcomed the time we spent at Grandma's table eating everything *except* oatmeal. We could always count on waffles or pancakes. This was a big deal. Just locating the waffle iron evolved into a hide and seek type of activity. I think the only time Grandma used it was when we visited. Grandma always doubled the waffle recipe, not because we ate so many but because it took almost one whole batch before we actually produced edible waffles. The first few seemed to burn from either too much oil or from leaving the batter in the waffle iron too long. The next attempts usually had to be surgically removed from the contraption with a fork due to lack of enough oil. Occasionally we would finally create a few perfect waffles; other times we just gave up. But even when we gave up, Grandma never forced us to eat oatmeal; she meticulously customized pancakes from the waffle batter into any shape we could think of. Bears were her specialty. Today, because of these fond memories, each batch of pancakes made in my home contains at least one bear—complete with chocolate chip eyes and buttons. I knew I could always depend on Grandma to make a *real* breakfast.

● Breakfast During the Summer

As a family, our summer vacations consisted of visiting cousins in Montana and taking camping trips. My cousins called my sister and me the "skinny, city cousins." Not that we grew up in a big city—Milton, Washington, was no metropolis—but compared to Townsend, Montana, believe me, it was. I thought oatmeal would be obsolete in Townsend but quickly discovered that not only was oatmeal popular in Montana, but also cornmeal mush. Yuk! The grown-ups told us that if we finished our cornmeal mush we could have a bowl of cornflakes. No cornflake in the world was worth eating that stuff. Soon they quit offering the cornflakes. Even Dad confirmed our evaluation of the mush. "This stuff is awful!" he would whisper as he forced a spoonful into his mouth. Needless to say, after a trip to Townsend, Montana, oatmeal had a little more appeal to it.

Other memories of summer breakfasts that come to mind are from when our family ventured into the wilderness. No oatmeal on camping trips! We cooked over an open fire; my dad, an appliance businessman, took a lid off of an old clothes washing machine, turned it upside down, and clamped a set of pliers to it for the handle, creating a makeshift griddle. We thought Dad was ingenious, especially since oatmeal never touched the griddle. That washing machine lid held enough bacon and eggs for an army. Pancakes tasted the best after being cooked (fried, rather) in bacon grease. Each pancake had crispy brown edges and a flavor that comforted our souls and filled our stomachs. To us, camp-cooking was the epitome of tasty, satisfying breakfasts.

● Breakfast and the Next Generation

Most people grow up hearing about how "when I was your age, I had to walk ten miles to school in the snow, blah, blah, blah . . ." not "when I was a kid, all we ate was oatmeal." Yes, I ate oatmeal growing up. Too much in my opinion. And now as I recall the memory of that stiff mountain of glue placed before me every morning, I have discovered that no matter where you grow up, a basic food staple exists in every household. Mine just happened to be OATMEAL. My cousins ate cornmeal mush, my roommates in college ate cracked wheat. I'm just glad that it didn't put hair on my chest like my dad said it would.

Because I grew up on oatmeal, I vowed that when I had a family of my own, I wouldn't feed them oatmeal. I made it my mission to be the quintessence of gourmet breakfast chefs everywhere. I love pancakes. I love waffles. I love crumb cakes. I love French toast. I love creating breakfast feasts. Since I love all of these morning foods so much, I make pancakes, waffles, crumb cakes, and French toast continually. In fact, I love breakfast so much that I have caused my own children to generate their own question: "Can't we just have cereal?" I can't fathom anyone wanting "just cereal" when the options are endless. Although I admit that, now, as an adult, I actually like oatmeal, especially when it's hot—not cold and stiff.

Hopefully *Beyond Oatmeal: 101 Breakfast Recipes* will fill your stomachs and your souls and take you back to your fond childhood memories of breakfasts past. Yes, there is more to breakfast than just oatmeal—much more.

And just in case you are curious and want to know how it all started, I have included the infamous oatmeal recipe at the end of this book. Enjoy!

Streusels and Crumb Cakes

Streusels and Crumb Cakes

Streusel and crumb cakes rank high among the most satisfying of home-baked goods. Unlike other cakes, crumb cakes can be served for breakfast, brunch, lunch, and after-dinner desserts, or at bridal or baby showers. Their crumbly topping and delicate, homey taste and smell are irresistible. The word *streusel* is German, meaning "sprinkle." Thus, streusel toppings usually contain flour, sugar, butter, and various spices all mixed together and sprinkled on top of a cake. Because of their many possible flavors, they are perfect for leisurely weekend mornings and any special occasion. The smell that wafts from the kitchen when a crumb cake comes out of the oven tantalizes the taste buds before the cake even passes the lips; it doesn't get any better than this.

● Crumb Cake Tips

Use regular stick margarine or butter. Reduced-fat products will make the finished product dry and tough. Low-fat margarine contains a higher air and water content that is released during baking and alters the consistency of the finished product.

Use a pastry blender or two table knives to cut the margarine or butter into the flour-sugar mixture. If you use your fingers, the heat from your hands can warm the margarine or butter and interfere with crumb formation. All fats used for cakes should be room temperature for the best results. If not, they will not blend well with the other ingredients.

Use flour to dust nuts, raisins, and chopped fruits before adding them to the batter to prevent them from sinking to the bottom of the cakes. For dustings, use flour from the measured flour in the recipe before adding any other ingredients, such as baking soda or baking powder.

Use your fingers to test for doneness by gently pressing the top of the cake. If it springs back fully when touched lightly in the center, the cake is ready to be removed from the oven.

Use 1½ teaspoons vinegar or lemon juice plus enough milk to make ½ cup if you need a substitution for a ½ cup of buttermilk.

Always remember to store baked goods in the refrigerator if they have cheese fillings

All flour is all-purpose unless otherwise noted.

Apple-Oatmeal Crumb Cake

An apple-oatmeal crumb cake with the home-style flavor baked right in. A wonderfully moist cake with a layer of apples and streusel. The addition of oatmeal gives a chewy contrast to the crispy, sugary topping.

Note: Any firm cooking apple can be used for this recipe.

1 cup flour
1/3 cup rolled oats
1/3 cup sugar
1/3 cup brown sugar, packed
1/8 tsp. salt
1/8 tsp. ground nutmeg
1/4 cup margarine or butter,
    cut into small pieces
1/4 tsp. baking soda
1/2 tsp. baking powder
1/3 cup apple juice
1 tsp. vanilla
1 large egg
1½ cups apple, chopped
    and peeled

Preheat oven to 350°F.

Lightly spoon flour into dry measuring cup and level with a knife. Combine the flour, oats, sugar, brown sugar, salt, and nutmeg in a bowl and cut in the margarine with a pastry blender until the mixture resembles coarse meal. Reserve ½ cup of flour mixture for topping and set aside.

Combine remaining flour mixture, baking powder, and baking soda and add the apple juice, vanilla, and egg.

Beat mixture at medium speed until blended and fold in chopped apple.

Spoon batter into a greased 8-inch round cake pan and sprinkle the reserved ½ cup flour mixture over batter. Bake at 350°F for 30 minutes or until cake springs back when touched lightly in center.

Cool cake on a wire rack. Makes 8 servings.

Autumn Apple Cake

This sweet autumn cake, filled with apple pieces and raisins,
is perfect to start off a cold fall morning.

4 Tbsp. butter, softened

6 Tbsp. sugar

1 egg, beaten

1 cup flour, sifted

2 cooking apples, peeled, cored, and sliced

⅓ cup raisins

Topping:

¾ cup flour

½ tsp. cinnamon

3 Tbsp. butter

2 Tbsp. sugar

Preheat the oven 350°F. Grease a deep 7-inch spingform pan; line the base with wax paper and grease the paper. To make the topping, sift the flour and cinnamon into a mixing bowl. Cut the butter into flour mixture until it resembles bread crumbs, then stir in the sugar. Set aside.

To make the base, put butter, sugar, egg, and flour into a bowl and beat 1 to 2 minutes until smooth. Spoon into prepared pan.

Mix together the apple slices and raisins and spread them evenly over the top. Sprinkle with topping.

Bake 1 hour. Cool in the pan for 10 minutes before turning out onto a wire rack, carefully peel off wax paper.

Optional: Decorate with slices of red dessert apple, and sprinkle with cinnamon and sugar. Serve warm or cool. Serves 8.

Apricot Cream Cake

Spring is in the air and apricots are a great way to celebrate its coming.
Soft color and a fresh, light flavor complete the canvas.

Cake:
1 (15 oz.) can apricot halves,
    drained; reserve 1 Tbsp. juice
1¼ cups flour
½ cup sugar
½ cup butter, softened
½ cup sour cream
2 eggs
1 tsp. baking powder
1 tsp. grated lemon peel

Topping:
⅓ cup sugar
2 Tbsp. butter
2 Tbsp. flour
1 tsp. grated lemon peel

Glaze:
½ cup powdered sugar
1 Tbsp. reserved apricot juice

Preheat oven to 350°F. Pat apricots dry with paper towels; cut into slices. Set aside.

Cake: Combine flour, sugar, butter, sour cream, eggs, baking powder, and lemon peel in large mixing bowl. Beat 1 to 2 minutes at low speed until well mixed, scraping sides occasionally. Spread into greased 8-inch square baking pan.

Topping: In small bowl, stir together sugar, butter, flour and lemon peel until crumbly. Arrange apricots over batter; spoon crumbly mixture over apricots.

Bake 40 to 50 minutes or until golden brown and toothpick inserted in center comes out clean.

Glaze: In another small bowl, stir together powdered sugar and enough reserved apricot juice (about 1 tablespoon) for desired glazing consistency. Drizzle over warm cake.

Tropical Banana Crumb Cake

The rich, toasted coconut crumb topping provides a perfect balance
of texture and flavor for this moist banana cake.

Cake:

1¼ cups flour

⅓ cup sugar

⅓ cup dark brown sugar, packed

¼ tsp. ground allspice

⅛ tsp. salt

¼ cup margarine or butter, cut into small pieces

½ tsp. baking soda

¾ tsp. baking powder

½ cup (1 medium) ripe banana, mashed

3 Tbsp. milk

1 egg

Topping:

¼ cup flaked, sweetened coconut

1 tsp. water

(½ cup reserved flour mixture)

Preheat oven to 350°F.

Cake: Lightly spoon flour into dry measuring cup and level with a knife. Combine flour, sugars, allspice, and salt in a bowl; cut in margarine until mixture resembles coarse meal. Reserve ½ cup flour mixture for topping; set aside.

Combine remaining flour mixture, baking soda, baking powder, banana, milk, and egg. Beat at medium speed with a mixer until blended. Spoon batter into a greased 8-inch round cake pan.

Topping: Combine reserved ½ cup flour mixture, coconut, and water; stir with a fork. Sprinkle crumb mixture over batter.

Bake at 350°F for 30 minutes or until cake springs back when touched lightly in center. Cool on a wire rack.

Banana Bran Delight

*Moist and chewy, this sweet cake is a good choice for
anyone looking for something a little more healthy.*

Cake:
1 egg
½ cup milk
3 Tbsp. vegetable oil
1½ cups bran flakes cereal
½ cup mashed ripe banana
1¼ cups flour
¼ cup packed brown sugar
¼ tsp. baking soda
½ tsp. cinnamon
2 tsp. baking powder
¼ tsp. salt
½ cup raisins

Topping:
1 Tbsp. butter
2 Tbsp. brown sugar
⅛ tsp. cinnamon

Preheat oven to 350°F. Grease a 9-inch round cake pan.

Cake: In medium bowl, combine egg, milk, and oil; beat until well blended. Stir in cereal and mashed banana until well mixed. Set aside.

In large bowl, combine flour, brown sugar, baking soda, cinnamon, baking powder, and salt; mix well. Stir in raisins. Add banana mixture; stir just until dry ingredients are moistened. Spread batter evenly in greased pan.

Topping: In small bowl, combine all topping ingredients; mix well. Sprinkle over batter.

Bake at 350°F for 25 to 35 minutes or until cake springs back when touched lightly in center. Cool 15 minutes. Serve warm.

Pear-berry Crumb Cake

This recipe was inspired by my original fruit pie I entered in the Western Washington Fair. The pear, together with the blackberry, provides both a smooth texture and a wonderful flavor.

Streusel Topping:
⅔ cup brown sugar, packed
½ cup flour
1 tsp. cinnamon
¼ tsp. nutmeg
4 Tbsp. butter
⅔ cup almonds, sliced

Cake:
2½ cups flour
1½ tsp. baking powder
½ tsp. baking soda
½ tsp. salt
1¼ cups sugar
6 Tbsp. butter, softened
2 eggs
1½ tsp. vanilla
1⅓ cups sour cream
2 cups pears, diced, divided
1 cup fresh blackberries;
   if frozen, thaw and drain
   thoroughly

Preheat oven to 350°F. Grease and flour a 9x13 baking pan.

Streusel: In medium bowl, mix brown sugar, flour, cinnamon, and nutmeg with fork until well blended. Work in butter with fingertips until evenly distributed. Add almonds and toss to mix; set aside.

Cake: In separate medium bowl, combine flour, baking powder, baking soda, and salt; set aside.

In large bowl, beat sugar with butter at low speed until blended, scraping bowl often. Increase speed to high; beat until creamy, about 2 minutes, occasionally scraping bowl. Reduce speed to low; add eggs, 1 at a time, beating well after each addition. Beat in vanilla.

On low speed, alternately add flour mixture and sour cream until batter is smooth, scraping bowl occasionally. With rubber spatula, fold in 1 cup pears. Spoon batter into pan; spread evenly. Mix remaining pears and blackberries together. Spoon over batter. Sprinkle top with streusel mixture.

Bake cake until toothpick inserted in center comes out clean, about 45 to 50 minutes. Cool cake in pan on wire rack one hour and serve warm.

Northwest Apple Cake

Two Northwest favorites are combined in this cake.
Sweet, tart, vibrant, and crunchy—no matter how you slice them, apples are an inviting addition.

Note: Any soft berry, such as raspberries, loganberries, or blueberries, can be used in place of blackberries.

¾ cup butter, softened
1 cup sugar (reserve 2 Tbsp.)
3 eggs
1½ cups self-rising flour
2 cups blackberries (or your choice of soft berries)
2 apples, peeled, cored, and grated

Preheat the oven to 350°F. Line the bottom of a 9-inch round or square cake pan with wax paper and grease it with butter.

Reserve 2 tablespoons sugar. Cream the butter with the remaining sugar in a large bowl until almost white, then beat in the eggs one at a time until thoroughly mixed. Fold in flour. Spoon about two-thirds of batter into prepared pan.

Mix together blackberries, apples, and reserved sugar. Spoon this over cake batter and then evenly distribute spoonfuls of the remaining cake batter over the fruit mixture.

Bake until golden and just firm to the touch, about one hour. Let cool in pan.

Blueberry Polka Dots

Blueberry lovers will go crazy for this one.
The poppy seeds add just the right amount of crunch!

Cake:
²/₃ cup sugar
½ cup butter
2 tsp. grated lemon peel
1 egg
1½ cups flour
2 Tbsp. poppy seeds
¼ tsp. salt
½ tsp. baking soda
½ cup sour cream

Filling:
2 cups blueberries (fresh or
    frozen)
2 tsp. flour
¼ tsp. ground nutmeg
⅓ cup sugar

Glaze:
⅓ cup powdered sugar
1 to 2 tsp. milk

Preheat oven to 350°F.

Cake: Grease and flour a 9- or 10-inch springform pan or line a round 9-inch cake pan with wax paper. In large bowl, combine sugar and butter; beat until light and fluffy. Add lemon peel and egg; beat two more minutes at medium speed.

In separate bowl, combine flour, poppy seeds, salt, and baking soda; mix well. Add the dry mixture to the butter mixture alternately with sour cream, beating well after each addition. Then spread the batter over the bottom and 1 inch up the side of the baking pan.

Filling: In large bowl, combine all filling ingredients; mix well and spoon over batter.

Bake at 350°F for 45 to 55 minutes, or until crust is golden brown.

Glaze: In small bowl, blend powdered sugar and milk until creamy. Pour over warm cake. Serves 8.

Toasted Almond Cherry Confection

This toasted almond and cherry cake will make you question why you don't eat like this more often.
It is definitely a morning treat to indulge in.

Cake:
½ cup butter, softened
1 cup sugar (reserve 6 Tbsp.)
3 eggs
1¼ cups flour
1⅓ cups ground almonds
1½ cups candied cherries,
    quartered

Topping:
reserved 6 Tbsp. sugar
⅓ cup sliced almonds

Preheat oven to 350°F. Grease an 8-inch round cake pan with butter and line the bottom and sides with a double thickness of wax paper.

In a bowl, cream the butter and sugar (except reserved 6 tablespoons) until almost white. Beat in first 2 eggs, one at a time. Separate the third egg and add the yolk to the creamed mixture and reserve the white for the topping.

Combine flour, half of ground almonds, and cherries, and fold into creamed mixture.

Pour into prepared pan and level the batter.

Topping: Combine the reserved 6 tablespoons sugar and remaining sliced almonds. Sprinkle on top of the cake.

Bake 60 to 75 minutes or until golden brown and a knife inserted in the center comes out clean. Let the cake cool in the pan, about 1 hour. Unmold on a wire rack.

Tip: When using candied cherries, it's a good idea to rinse and dry them to remove any excess sugar syrup. Then powder them with flour. This will help prevent the cherries from sinking to the bottom of the cake during baking.

Classic Crumb Cake

*This light, moist cake with a wonderful cinnamon butter crumb topping
is an original, traditional crumb cake.*

1¼ cups flour

⅔ cup packed brown sugar

1 tsp. cinnamon

½ tsp. nutmeg

⅛ tsp. salt

¼ cup margarine or butter, cut
   into small pieces

½ tsp. baking soda

½ tsp. baking powder

½ cup buttermilk

1 tsp. vanilla extract

1 large egg

Preheat oven to 350°F.

Lightly spoon flour into dry measuring cups and level with a knife. Combine the flour, brown sugar, cinnamon, nutmeg, and salt in a bowl and cut in margarine with a pastry blender until the mixture resembles coarse meal. Reserve ½ cup of flour mixture for the topping and set aside.

In medium bowl, combine remaining flour mixture, baking soda, and baking powder. Then add the buttermilk, vanilla, and egg to the dry mixture.

Beat at medium speed until blended. Spoon batter into a greased 8-inch round cake pan.

Sprinkle reserved ½ cup flour mixture over batter.

Bake at 350°F for 30 minutes or until cake springs back when touched lightly in center. Cool on a wire rack. Serves 8.

Instant Gratification

Chocolate is not just for dessert anymore. Why not have chocolate for breakfast? Start your day by treating yourself. Finally have dessert first. Make sure you have plenty of cold milk on hand.

Note: A creamy chocolate glaze is drizzled over this irresistible crumb cake.

Streusel Topping:
½ cup brown sugar, packed
½ cup flour
¼ cup butter or margarine
¾ cup sliced almonds
½ cup chocolate chips

Cake:
2 cups flour
1 tsp. baking soda
1 tsp. baking powder
½ tsp. salt
¾ cup butter or margarine, softened
¾ cup brown sugar, packed
¼ cup honey
1 tsp. almond extract
3 large eggs
½ cup milk
1 cup chocolate chips

Glaze:
1 Tbsp. butter or margarine
½ cup chocolate chips
1 Tbsp. milk

Preheat oven to 350°F. Grease and flour two 9-inch round cake pans.

Streusel: Combine brown sugar and flour in medium bowl. Cut in butter or margarine with pastry blender; blend well until mixture resembles coarse crumbs. Stir in sliced almonds and chocolate chips. Set aside.

Cake: Combine flour, baking soda, baking powder, and salt in small bowl. In a separate bowl, beat butter, brown sugar, honey, and almond extract until creamy. Add the eggs one at a time, beating well after each addition. Gradually beat in flour mixture, alternating with milk. Stir in 1 cup chocolate chips. Divide batter into prepared cake pans and sprinkle with streusel topping.

Bake 20 to 30 minutes or until a toothpick inserted in center comes out clean. Cool in pans for 10 minutes. Make glaze while cake is baking. Drizzle cooled cake with glaze.

Chocolate Glaze: Melt remaining ½ cup chocolate chips, butter, and milk in small, heavy-duty saucepan over low heat, stirring until smooth.

Buttermilk Special

This moist crumb cake tastes like homemade buttermilk
doughnuts rolled in sugar and cinnamon. However, it's much easier to make.

Note: Since the recipe Makes 2 cakes, serve one now and one later.

Crumb Topping:

2 cups flour

½ cup sugar

½ cup packed brown sugar

2 tsp. cinnamon

1 cup margarine or butter, softened

Cake:

2¼ cups flour

2¼ tsp. baking powder

½ tsp. salt

1¼ cups sugar

½ cup margarine or butter, softened

3 large eggs

¾ cup milk

2 tsp. vanilla

Preheat oven to 350°F. Grease two 9-inch round cake pans; dust with flour.

Crumb Topping: In medium bowl, mix flour, sugar, brown sugar, and cinnamon until well blended. With pastry blender or fingertips, work in margarine or butter until evenly distributed; set aside.

Cake: In another medium bowl, mix flour, baking powder, and salt; set aside.

In large bowl, beat sugar with margarine or butter at low speed until blended, scraping bowl often with rubber spatula. Increase speed to medium; beat until well mixed, about 2 minutes, scraping bowl occasionally.

Reduce speed to low; add eggs, 1 at a time, beating well after each addition.

In small bowl, combine milk and vanilla. With mixer at low speed, alternately add flour mixture and milk mixture, beginning and ending with flour mixture, until batter is smooth, scraping bowl occasionally.

Pour batter into pans. Press crumb topping into large chunks; sprinkle evenly over batter. Bake cakes 40 to 45 minutes, or until toothpick inserted in center comes

out clean. Cool cakes in pans on wire racks for about 15 minutes. With small metal spatula, loosen the cakes from the sides of the pans. Invert onto plates, then immediately invert back to crumb side up onto wire racks to cool completely.

Makes 2 crumb cakes. Makes 10 servings per cake.

Double Blueberry Morning Cake

Lemonade adds zip to this tender blueberry-laced cake. The blueberry sauce tops it off perfectly.

Cake:
3 cups cake flour
2½ tsp. baking powder
¼ tsp. salt
1¼ cups butter, softened
1¾ cups sugar
4 eggs
1 Tbsp. grated lemon peel
2 tsp. vanilla
1 cup lemonade
1½ cups blueberries

Blueberry Sauce:
1 cup blueberries
¼ cup sugar
2 tsp. cornstarch
¼ cup water

Preheat oven to 350°F. Grease a 10-inch Bundt pan.

Cake: In small bowl, sift together cake flour, baking powder, and salt. In large bowl beat the butter until creamy. Beat in the sugar until light and fluffy, approximately 2 to 3 minutes. Add eggs, one at a time, beating well each time. Then beat in lemon peel and vanilla.

Beat flour mixture into butter mixture in 3 additions, alternating with lemonade and ending with flour mixture. Fold in blueberries. Pour into prepared pan.

Bake in preheated 350°F oven 45 to 50 minutes or until the top is golden and a knife inserted in center of cake comes out clean. Place cake on wire rack to cool.

Sauce: Combine blueberries, sugar, cornstarch, and water in saucepan. Cook over medium heat until sugar is dissolved, liquid is no longer cloudy, and blueberries begin to burst, about 5 to 7 minutes. Puree in blender or food processor until smooth.

To serve, cut cake into slices and drizzle with warm blueberry sauce.

Gingerbread Crumb Cake

*A great holiday breakfast treat. Warm gingerbread fills the air
with the comforting aroma of spices and molasses.*

1 cup flour
2/3 cup sugar
1/2 tsp. ground ginger
1/2 tsp. cinnamon
1/4 tsp. ground nutmeg
1/8 tsp. salt
1/8 tsp. ground cloves
1/4 cup margarine or butter, cut
    into pieces
1/2 tsp. baking soda
1/2 tsp. baking powder
1/2 cup buttermilk
2 Tbsp. molasses
1 large egg
1½ tsp. water

Preheat oven to 350°F.

Lightly spoon flour into dry measuring cup and level with a knife. In a bowl, combine flour, sugar, ginger, cinnamon, nutmeg, salt, and cloves and cut in margarine with a pastry blender until mixture resembles coarse meal. Reserve ½ cup flour mixture; set aside.

Combine the remaining flour mixture, baking soda, and baking powder. Add the buttermilk, molasses, and egg to flour mixture.

Beat at medium speed until blended. Spoon into a greased 8-inch round cake pan. Combine reserved ½ cup flour mixture and water; stir with a fork. Sprinkle over batter.

Bake at 350°F for 30 minutes. Cool on a wire rack. Serves 8.

Graham Cracker Cake

*A perfect graham cracker cookie taste makes the sweet vanilla grahams
and the nutty flavor of chopped pecans an irresistible combination.*

Crumb Mixture:

8 squares or ¾ cup graham
   crackers, crushed
¼ cup pecans, chopped
2 Tbsp. brown sugar, packed
½ tsp. cinnamon
3 Tbsp. butter, melted

Cake:

½ cup butter, softened
¼ cup sugar
½ tsp. vanilla
½ tsp. lemon peel, grated
1 cup flour
½ tsp. baking soda
½ tsp. baking powder
½ cup sour cream

Preheat oven to 350°F. Grease an 8-inch round cake pan and set aside.

Crumb mixture: Crush enough graham crackers to make ¾ cup. Combine graham cracker crumbs, pecans, brown sugar, and cinnamon in a small bowl. Add the melted butter; stir until well blended.

Cake: Cream softened butter and sugar in large bowl with electric mixer at medium speed until light and fluffy. Beat in the vanilla and lemon peel and set aside.

Sift together the flour, baking soda, and baking powder in a medium six bowl. Add the flour mixture and sour cream alternately to the sugar mixture, beating well after each addition.

Spoon half of the batter into prepared pan, spreading evenly. Sprinkle ⅔ of the crumb mixture evenly over batter. Spoon remaining batter over crumbs and top with the remaining crumb mixture.

Bake for 30 to 35 minutes or until toothpick inserted into center comes out clean. Let cool 10 minutes before removing from the pan.

Lemon Crumb Cake

*This refreshing lemon-topped cake is a wonderful
choice for a late morning brunch or an afternoon bridal shower.*

Cake:
1¾ cups flour
2 tsp. baking powder
1 tsp. cinnamon,
5 Tbsp. margarine, softened
¾ cup sugar
2 eggs
1 tsp. vanilla
½ cup milk

Filling:
1 (21 oz.) can lemon pie filling

Streusel Topping:
½ cup flour
¼ cup sugar
1 tsp. cinnamon
1 tsp. margarine, softened
1 tsp. water

Cake: In medium bowl, combine flour, baking powder, and cinnamon; set aside.

In large bowl, beat margarine and ¾ cup sugar at high speed until creamy. Blend in eggs and vanilla. On low speed, gradually add flour mixture alternately with milk until well combined. Spread the batter into a greased, 9-inch springform pan.

Filling: Spoon lemon pie filling over batter. Bake at 350°F for 40 minutes.

Topping: While cake is baking, make streusel topping by combining flour, remaining sugar, and cinnamon. Cut in margarine until mixture resembles coarse crumbs. Stir in water.

Remove cake from oven and sprinkle streusel topping onto the top of the half baked cake. Return cake to oven and bake 15 to 20 minutes more or until toothpick inserted in center comes out clean. Cool in pan or on wire rack for 25 minutes. Remove outside ring of pan; serve warm.

Lemon-Coconut Layered Cake

A great way to wake up your taste buds. If desired,
toast the coconut before stirring it into the streusel mixture.

Streusel:
½ cup flour
⅓ cup sugar
3 Tbsp. butter
½ cup coconut

Cake:
2¼ cups flour
1 cup sugar
½ tsp. baking soda
½ tsp. baking powder
½ tsp. salt
¾ cup butter, softened
⅔ cup vanilla yogurt
1 Tbsp. lemon juice
2 tsp. grated lemon peel
1 egg
1 egg yolk

Filling:
½ cup lemon pie filling

Glaze:
½ cup powdered sugar
1 tsp. lemon juice
1 tsp. water

Preheat oven to 350°F. Grease and flour 9- or 10-inch springform pan.

Streusel: in medium bowl, combine ½ cup flour and ⅓ cup sugar. Mix well. With fork, cut in 3 tablespoons butter until mixture resembles coarse crumbs. Stir in coconut. Set aside.

Cake: In large bowl, combine flour, sugar, baking soda, baking powder, and salt; mix well. Add butter, yogurt, lemon juice, lemon peel, egg, and egg yolk; stir with spoon until well blended. Spread 2 cups of batter in greased and floured pan. Sprinkle with ¾ cup of the streusel.

Filling: Drop lemon pie filling onto top of streusel mixture by ½ teaspoonfuls within ½ inch of the pan edge. Spoon remaining batter over lemon mixture. Sprinkle with remaining streusel.

Bake at 350°F for 50 to 60 minutes or until toothpick inserted in center comes out clean. Cool 15 minutes; remove sides of pan.

Glaze: Combine glaze ingredients; stir until smooth. Drizzle over warm streusel cake.

Rosemary Cake

The robust flavor of fresh rosemary combined with the tangy lemon makes this crumb cake incredibly versatile.
Serve alone or with fresh fruit for breakfast or an afternoon snack.

Note: Rosemary is an herb in the mint family.

Cake:

1¼ cups flour
⅔ cup sugar
⅛ tsp. salt
¼ cup margarine or butter, chilled and cut into pieces
¾ tsp. fresh rosemary (or ¼ tsp. dried)
¼ tsp. baking soda
½ tsp. baking powder
⅓ cup buttermilk
2 Tbsp. lemon juice
1 large egg

Topping:

2 tsp. grated lemon rind
¾ tsp. water
rosemary sprigs (optional)
lemon slices (optional)

Preheat oven to 350°F.

Cake: Lightly spoon flour into dry measuring cups and level with a knife. Combine flour, sugar, and salt in a bowl and cut in margarine with a pastry blender until mixture resembles coarse meal. Reserve ½ cup flour mixture for topping and set aside.

Combine remaining flour mixture, rosemary, baking soda and baking powder; add buttermilk, lemon juice, and egg.

Beat at medium speed until blended. Spoon batter into a greased 8-inch round cake pan.

Topping: Combine reserved ½ cup flour mixture, lemon rind, and water; stir with a fork. Sprinkle the crumb mixture over batter. Bake at 350°F for 30 minutes. Cool on a wire rack and garnish with rosemary sprigs and lemon slices, if desired. Serves 8.

Simple Lemon Creme Cake

*Your friends and family will rave that you worked so
hard, but don't tell them it was so simple—enjoy the moment!*

Cake:

1 cup flour
½ cup sugar
1 tsp. baking powder
¼ tsp. baking soda
¼ cup margarine, soft
1 pkg. cream cheese
¼ milk
1 tsp. grated lemon peel
1 egg
¼ cup raspberry jam

Frosting:

½ cup powdered sugar
1 tsp. lemon juice
2 tsp. margarine, softened
¼ cup sliced almonds

Preheat oven to 350°F.

Cake: In medium bowl, cream margarine and cream cheese with mixer. Add flour, sugar, baking powder, and baking soda; mix well. Add milk, lemon peel, and egg; stir. Pour mixture into greased and floured 8-inch square pan. Using a spoon, carefully swirl in raspberry jam—do not over mix.

Bake at 350°F for 25 to 30 minutes.

Frosting: While cake is baking, mix powered sugar, lemon juice, and margarine together.

Remove cake from oven and cool on wire rack. Drizzle frosting over top of cooled cake. Sprinkle with sliced almonds.

Orange Sunshine Cake

California or bust! Orange juice has never been more welcome.
This is a light yet rich tasting breakfast cake. Serve topped with fresh whipped cream.

1 cup whole wheat flour
1 cup flour
2 tsp. baking soda
4 Tbsp. butter
1 cup sugar
3 medium eggs
2 cups orange juice
2 tsp. orange zest
powdered sugar

Preheat oven to 350°F. Lightly grease a Bundt pan.

In large bowl, combine whole wheat flour, white flour, and baking soda. Add eggs one at a time; beat after each addition.

Boil orange juice and orange zest. Chill just until cool to the touch. Add juice to flour mixture and mix. Beat butter and sugar together. Blend into flour and juice mixture.

Pour into pan and bake for 35 to 40 minutes or until toothpick comes out clean. Cool on rack and invert. Sprinkle with powdered sugar before serving.

Overnight Buttermilk Cake

Here's a great recipe when you want a special breakfast but anticipate a rushed morning. Mix up the cake batter and refrigerate it in the pan overnight, then pop it in the oven in the morning. Quick and simple!

Cake:
1 cup flour
¼ cup sugar
¼ cup brown sugar, packed
½ tsp. baking soda
1 tsp. baking powder
¼ tsp. salt
½ cup buttermilk
⅓ cup shortening
1 egg

Topping:
¼ cup brown sugar, packed
¼ cup chopped nuts
¼ tsp. ground nutmeg

Grease and flour 9-inch round or square pan.

Cake: In small bowl, combine all cake ingredients; blend at low speed until moistened. Beat 2 minutes at medium speed. Pour batter into pan.

Topping: In small bowl, combine all topping ingredients; blend well and sprinkle over batter. Cover and refrigerate at least 8 hours.

Preheat oven to 350°F. Uncover cake and bake 25 to 35 minutes or until toothpick inserted in center comes out clean. Serve warm.

Blueberry Peach Cake

Not just a summer splurge, this cake can be made any time of the year.

Note: Canned fruit also works great in this recipe since the fruit will become soft when cooked.

Cake:
2 cups flour

1 cup sugar

2 tsp. baking powder

1 tsp. salt

1½ tsp. grated orange peel

½ cup butter

1 cup milk

1 tsp. vanilla

2 eggs, slightly beaten

1 cup fresh or frozen peaches, sliced and thawed

1 cup fresh or frozen blueberries, thawed

Glaze:
1 cup powdered sugar

¼ tsp. almond extract

3–5 tsp. milk

Preheat oven to 350°F. Grease 13x9-inch pan.

Cake: In large bowl, combine flour, sugar, baking powder, salt, and orange peel; mix well. With fork, cut in butter until crumbly.

Add milk, vanilla, and eggs; stir just until dry ingredients are moistened. Pour 2¼ cups of batter into greased pan.

Top with peaches and blueberries. Spread remaining batter over fruit.

Bake at 350°F for 35 to 45 minutes or until edges are golden brown. Cool 20 minutes.

Glaze: In small bowl, blend glaze ingredients, adding enough milk for desired drizzling consistency. Drizzle over cake.

Razzy Peach Crisp

If I had to choose a favorite berry, it would definitely be the raspberry.
Sweet and tart and so versatile.

Crumb Topping:

¾ cup flour
¼ cup brown sugar
¼ cup sugar
¾ tsp. cinnamon
¼ cup pecans or walnuts,
    chopped
6 Tbsp. butter, melted

Filling:

¼ cup sugar
2 tsp. cornstarch
7 cups fresh peaches, sliced
½ pint fresh raspberries
whipped topping

Preheat oven to 375°F.

Topping: In medium bowl, combine flour, sugars, cinnamon, and chopped walnuts. Add butter and mix until crumbly; set aside.

Filling: mix sugar and cornstarch; set aside.

In large bowl, toss sliced peaches with cornstarch mixture until evenly coated.

Gently stir in raspberries. Spoon fruit mixture into a 4-quart baking dish; sprinkle evenly with crumble topping.

Bake 25 to 30 minutes or until peaches are tender and topping is golden brown. Serve warm with ice cream or whipped topping.

Raspberry Perfection

A simple, easy-to-make crumb cake. Apricot preserves go equally well with the cream cheese filling and sliced almonds.

Crumb Mixture:
2¼ cups flour
¾ cup sugar
¾ cup butter

Crumb Batter:
½ tsp. baking soda
½ tsp. baking powder
¼ tsp. salt
¾ cup sour cream
1 tsp. almond extract
1 egg

Filling:
1 (8 oz.) pkg. cream cheese,
  softened
¼ cup sugar
1 egg
½ cup raspberry preserves
½ cup sliced almonds

Preheat oven to 350°F. Grease and flour bottom and sides of a 9- or 10-inch springform pan.

Crumb Mixture: In large bowl, make crumb mixture by combining flour and sugar; mix well. With a fork, cut in butter until mixture resembles coarse crumbs. Reserve 1 cup crumb mixture.

Crumb Batter: Add baking soda, baking powder, salt, sour cream, almond extract, and egg to remaining crumb mixture; blend well. Spread batter over bottom and 2 inches up sides of pan.

Filling: In small bowl, combine cream cheese, sugar, and egg; blend well. Pour into batter-lined pan. Carefully spoon raspberry preserves evenly over cream cheese mixture.

In small bowl, combine reserved crumb mixture and sliced almonds. Sprinkle over preserves.

Bake at 350°F for 45 minutes or until cream cheese filling is set and crust is a deep golden brown. Cool 15 minutes; remove sides of pan.

Simple Raspberry Indulgence

A slightly tart cake with a crunchy-textured top.
Use your imagination and substitute the raspberry jam for another fruit jam. The possibilities are endless.

Cake:
1 cup flour
⅓ cup sugar
⅛ tsp. salt
¼ cup chilled margarine or
    butter, cut into small pieces
½ tsp. baking powder
¼ tsp. baking soda
⅓ cup sour cream
2 Tbsp. milk
1 tsp. vanilla
½ tsp. almond extract
1 large egg

Topping:
3 oz. cream cheese, softened
2 Tbsp. sugar
1 egg white
¼ cup raspberry jam
2 Tbsp. sliced almonds

Preheat oven to 350°F.

Cake: Lightly spoon flour into dry measuring cup and level with a knife. Combine flour, sugar, and salt in a bowl; cut in margarine with a pastry blender until mixture resembles coarse meal. Reserve ½ cup flour mixture for topping; set aside.

Combine remaining flour mixture, baking powder, and baking soda; then add sour cream, milk, vanilla, almond extract, and egg. Beat at medium speed until blended. Spoon batter into greased, 8-inch round cake pan.

Topping: Combine cream cheese, sugar, and egg white; beat at medium speed until blended. Spread evenly over batter; dot with preserves. Top with raspberry jam. Combine the reserved ½ cup flour mixture and almonds and sprinkle crumb mixture over jam.

Bake at 350°F for 30 minutes or until cake springs back when touched lightly in center. Cool on a wire rack. Serves 8.

Quick Picnic Crumb Cake

This moist, tender crumb cake is a classic and a good choice when you need something sweet to take to a friend or neighbor. Watch out—you might suddenly acquire lots of new friends!

Cake:
1 cup butter, softened
1½ cups sugar
3 eggs
1 tsp. vanilla
3 cups flour
2½ tsp. baking powder
1 tsp. salt
¼ tsp. baking soda
1 cup sour cream
½ cup milk

Filling:
2 cups pie filling or jam of your
    choice
1 cup slivered almonds

Preheat oven to 350°F. Grease and flour 12-cup Bundt pan.

Cake: In large bowl, combine butter and sugar; beat until light and fluffy. Add eggs one at a time, beating well after each addition. Add vanilla and mix well.

In large bowl, combine flour, baking powder, salt, and baking soda; mix well. Alternate adding flour mixture, sour cream, and milk to butter mixture until all is mixed well. Spoon half of batter into greased and floured pan.

Filling: Spoon filling over batter. Then spoon remaining batter over filling. Sprinkle almonds on top of cake.

Bake at 350°F for 50 to 60 minutes or until a knife inserted in the center comes out clean. Cool in pan for 10 minutes; invert onto wire rack. Cool at least 10 minutes.

Cinnamon-Sugar Walnut Cake

Nothing will get them out of bed and to the table quicker than the smell of a cinnamon and sugar cake baking in the oven. This is a moist, tender, and easy-to-make cake.

Filling:
4 Tbsp. butter, melted
½ cup brown sugar
1 Tbsp. cinnamon
1 Tbsp. flour
¼ cup walnuts, chopped

Cake:
1½ cups flour
1½ tsp. baking powder
½ tsp. salt
½ cup butter, softened
½ cup sugar
½ tsp. vanilla
1 egg
½ cup milk
¼ cup walnut pieces for topping

Preheat oven to 350°F. Grease an 8-inch square baking pan and set aside.

Filling: Mix butter, brown sugar, cinnamon, and flour in a small bowl; stir in walnuts and set aside.

Cake: Mix flour, baking powder, and salt in medium size bowl with a wire whisk until light and thoroughly combined.

Beat butter, sugar, and vanilla in large bowl until well mixed; beat in egg. Beat in flour mixture alternately with milk.

Spread half the batter into prepared pan. Spread evenly with filling mixture. Top with remaining batter, spreading to edges of pan. Top with walnuts.

Bake for about 45 to 50 minutes, or until toothpick inserted in the center comes out clean.

Cut into squares and serve warm. A nice pat of butter on top adds to the cake's irresistible flavor!

Naturally Heart Healthy

Maple syrup takes the place of the sugar in this cake. This is an attractive and rich cake, but not too sweet. Fully overflowing with plenty of flavor.

Cake:
½ cup flour
1 tsp. baking soda
½ tsp. salt
1¼ cups whole-wheat flour
1 egg
1 cup buttermilk
¼ cup butter, melted
½ cup maple syrup

Topping:
¼ cup whole-wheat flour
¼ cup brown sugar, packed
¾ cup granola
½ cup pecans or walnuts, chopped
1 tsp. cinnamon
4 Tbsp. butter, melted

Preheat oven to 375°F.

Sift together the white flour, baking soda, and salt.

Cake: Mix in the whole-wheat flour with a fork. In large bowl, beat the egg until very light; add the buttermilk, butter, and maple syrup and beat well to blend. Add the flour mixture and fold in gently until just combined. Spread batter smoothly in a greased 8-inch square pan.

Topping: Toss the flour, sugar, granola, pecans, and cinnamon with a fork. Drizzle butter over mixture and toss again. Sprinkle over batter.

Bake at 375°F about 25 minutes or until a toothpick inserted into the cake comes out clean. Serve warm with your favorite fruit topping.

Chocolate Morsel Crumb Cake

Chocolate and pecans complement each other perfectly in this delicious cake.
Be warned though—one piece will never be enough!

Cake:

3 cups flour, divided
⅓ cup sugar
1 tsp. salt
2 pkgs. rapid-rise dry yeast
½ cup water
½ cup milk
½ cup butter
2 eggs, beaten
¾ cup semi-sweet chocolate
    morsels

Topping:

½ cup butter
⅔ cup flour
⅔ cup sugar
2 tsp. cinnamon
1 cup semi-sweet chocolate
    morsels
1 cup pecans, chopped

Cake: In large bowl, combine 1 cup flour, sugar, salt, and dry yeast.

In a small sauce pan or microwavable bowl, heat water, milk, and butter until very warm. Be careful not to burn. Gradually add to dry ingredients. Beat 2 minutes at medium speed, scraping bowl occasionally. Add eggs and 1 cup flour; beat 2 minutes at high speed, scraping bowl occasionally. Stir in chocolate morsels and remaining 1 cup flour to make a soft batter.

Turn into greased 13x9-inch baking pan. Cover; let rise in warm place until doubled in size, about 1 hour.

Topping: In medium bowl, cut butter into flour until crumbly. Stir in sugar, cinnamon, semi-sweet chocolate morsels, and chopped pecans.

Bake cake at 400°F for 15 minutes; remove from oven and sprinkle with topping. Return to oven and bake additional 10 minutes. Remove from pan; cool on wire rack.

Holiday Pumpkin Crumb Cake

Pumpkin is not only for pies anymore. Serve this smooth pumpkin crumb cake for breakfast.
It will get every one's taste buds ready for the big turkey feast.

3 cups flour
2 tsp. baking soda
2 tsp. baking powder
1 Tbsp. cinnamon
1 tsp. salt
½ tsp. cloves
¼ tsp. allspice
¼ tsp. nutmeg
1 (16 oz.) can pumpkin
2 cups sugar
1¼ cups oil
4 eggs
1 cup nuts, chopped

Preheat oven to 350°F. Grease and flour sides and bottom of a springform pan. In medium size bowl, sift together flour, baking soda, baking powder, cinnamon, salt, cloves, allspice, and nutmeg.

In large bowl, beat together pumpkin, sugar, oil, and eggs, one at a time. Add flour mixture and chopped nuts to liquid mixture, stirring just until moistened. Pour into pan.

Bake in a preheated oven 40 minutes, or until toothpick inserted in center comes out clean. Let cool in pan for 10 minutes. Remove cake carefully from pan, dust with cinnamon, and serve with whipped cream. Makes 12 servings

Cranberry Walnut Crumb Cake

*The cranberries' refreshing tartness provides a distinctive
contrast to the nutty crumb topping.*

Cranberry Mixture:

2 cups dried cranberries
1 cup apple juice
½ cup brown sugar
½ cup water
1 tsp. cinnamon

Cake:

3 cups flour
1 cup sugar
1 cup walnuts, toasted and
  ground
1 tsp. cinnamon
2 tsp. baking powder
¼ tsp. salt
4 eggs, beaten
1 cup buttermilk
1 cup butter, melted
1½ tsp. vanilla

Streusel Topping:

⅔ cup flour
⅓ cup brown sugar, packed
¼ cup sugar
¾ tsp. cinnamon
¼ tsp. salt
½ tsp. vanilla
⅓ cup butter, softened

To toast walnuts, spread on ungreased pan. Bake in preheated 350°F oven 5 to 7 minutes, or until brown, stirring occasionally. When cool, place in food processor and process until finely ground.

Preheat oven to 325°F. Grease a 10-inch springform pan; set aside.

Cranberry Mixture: Combine cranberries, apple juice, brown sugar, water, and cinnamon. Bring to a boil in a small saucepan, stirring until sugar is dissolved. Remove from heat and cover pan; let stand 10 minutes. Drain cranberries, discarding liquid.

Cake: In large bowl, stir together all dry ingredients for the cake. In medium bowl, mix eggs, milk, butter, and vanilla. Add egg mixture to flour mixture, stirring until just moistened—do not over mix. Pour batter into prepared greased pan. Sprinkle cranberry mixture into center of batter, leaving 1 inch from the outer edge.

Topping: Combine flour, brown sugar, sugar, cinnamon, salt, and vanilla. Stir with a fork, add butter. Using a pastry blender, cut in butter until crumbly.

Sprinkle streusel topping over cake, completely covering entire cake top. Bake for 30 to 40 minutes. Cool on wire rack.

Pancakes

Pancakes

Pancakes are undeniably one of my many passions. I can't decide which I prefer more—making them or eating them.

Flipping pancakes for family, friends, campers, scouts, school parties, pajama parties, primary activities, and birthday brunches are only a small number of the many occasions in which I get the opportunity to make pancakes.

Any overnight guests that stay at my home receive my signature bear pancakes made with chocolate chip eyes and buttons. They always eat whatever I make. My kids will say, "Oh no! Mom's got someone to eat her pancakes." I'm sure some eat them out of duty or to be polite. But since the guests always ask for more, I know it's because they're good.

For those who don't want to try their hand at making pancake shapes, there are griddle forms that you place on your griddle and pour your batter into to create hearts, stars, sheep, dinosaurs and more. And yes, even a bear.

● Pancake Tips

Make sure the griddle is hot. A few drops of water sprinkled on the surface should dance.

Do not over mix the batter. Over mixing results in tough, flabby pancakes. Pancake batter should be mixed just until the wet and dry ingredients are combined. Don't worry about lumps. You want them. They'll cook out on the griddle.

A light coating of oil or non-stick spray at the start is all you need for most pancakes.

Don't let pancakes merge into each other, and avoid moving them while the first side is cooking—they'll brown more evenly if you leave them alone.

Do not flatten pancakes after turning them over.

Pancakes are ready to flip when their surface is covered with bubbles, their edges look dry, and a peek at their undersides reveals a golden brown color. Turn them gently, barely lifting them off the griddle.

Buttermilk Pancakes

This traditional pancake is popular for its ability to taste great
with just about any topping you can think of.

1¼ cups flour
1 egg
1¼ cups buttermilk
¼ cup sugar
1 tsp. baking powder
1 tsp. baking soda
¼ cup cooking oil
pinch of salt

Preheat a skillet over medium heat. Use a pan with a nonstick surface or apply a little nonstick spray.

In blender or with a mixer, combine ingredients until smooth.

Pour batter by spoonfuls into the hot pan, forming 5-inch circles. When the edges appear to harden, flip the pancake. Pancakes should be golden brown.

Cook pancakes on the other side for same amount of time until golden brown. Makes 8 to 10 pancakes.

Banana Party

Mashed bananas make these pancakes rich, tender, and moist.
They're great with assorted fresh fruit.

1¾ cups flour
1 Tbsp. sugar
1½ tsp. baking powder
½ tsp. salt
¼ tsp. cinnamon
2 eggs, slightly beaten
2 cups milk
2 ripe medium bananas,
　mashed
3 Tbsp. margarine, melted
⅓ cup pecans or walnuts, finely
　chopped

In mixing bowl, combine flour, sugar, baking powder, salt, and cinnamon. In another mixing bowl, combine eggs, milk, bananas, and margarine. Add to the flour mixture. Stir just until wet but still lumpy. Stir in nuts.

Heat a lightly greased griddle or heavy skillet over medium heat. For each pancake, pour about ¼ cup batter onto the hot griddle.

Cook until pancakes are golden brown, turning to cook second side when pancake surfaces are bubbly (about 1 to 2 minutes per side). Serve immediately. Makes 16 pancakes.

Whole Wheat Pancakes

The flavor just bursts out of these. Enjoy this morning classic any day of the week.

1¼ cups whole wheat flour,
  sifted
3 tsp. baking powder
¾ tsp. salt
3 Tbsp. brown sugar
3 eggs, well beaten
1¼ cups milk
3 Tbsp. cooking oil

Stir together dry ingredients. Combine eggs, milk, and oil; stir into flour mixture. Do not over beat. Bake on ungreased griddle until golden brown, then flip.

Serve warm with butter and maple syrup or fruit preserves.

Raspberry Valentine Pancakes

Your family will give you a perfect score every time you serve these beauties.
Be careful to gently fold in the berries.

1 cup flour
2 tsp. sugar
¼ tsp. baking soda
¼ tsp. salt
1 egg, beaten
1 cup buttermilk
1½ Tbsp. butter, melted
1 cup raspberries
powdered sugar

Have a hot, well-oiled griddle ready.

Sift together dry ingredients. In small bowl, combine egg, buttermilk, and butter, mixing well. Quickly stir into dry ingredients—do not over mix. Sprinkle the berries on top and fold in gently.

Place on the griddle by large spoonfuls. Cook until golden on the underside, about 2 to 3 minutes, then turn.

Cook another minute or so until done. Sprinkle with powdered sugar and serve. Makes 12 or more 3-inch pancakes.

Apple Flapjacks

Apple butter and whipped cream are a must for this flavorful pancake.
These would make even the legendary Johnny Appleseed proud.

1 cup flour
½ cup graham flour
1 Tbsp. sugar
½ tsp. cinnamon
1 tsp. baking powder
1 medium apple, finely chopped
2 eggs
1 Tbsp. oil
1 cup milk
apple butter
whipped cream

Heat a large skillet over medium heat.

In large bowl, blend together the flours, sugar, cinnamon, baking powder, and apple. Make a well in the center of the flour mixture and add eggs, oil, and milk. Stir until the ingredients are combined but still lumpy.

Brush the skillet with oil. Drop a heaping spoonful of the batter onto the prepared skillet and cook for 3 to 5 minutes or until bottom is golden brown and the top is speckled with holes. Turn and brown the other side.

Serve warm. Makes 14 to 16 pancakes.

Pancake Wedges

I like to call this the pizza pancake.
It's cooked as one large round pancake, and then cut and served in wedges.

2 large eggs
1 cup milk
¼ cup margarine, melted
½ tsp. vanilla
⅛ tsp. salt
6 slices stale white bread,
    crusts removed, diced

In medium bowl, beat eggs until foamy. Beat in milk, margarine, vanilla, and salt. Stir in bread pieces. Let mixture sit about 30 minutes.

When ready to cook, preheat a large skillet over medium heat and brush it with oil.

Pour all of the batter into the skillet at one time and cook until the bottom of the pancake is light brown. Using a large spatula, turn the pancake and cook on the other side until browned. Remove pan from heat and use a knife to cut the pancake into wedges.

Serve warm. Makes 4 to 6 servings.

Tip: Honey butter is great on this.

Golden Cornmeal Pancakes

A great, low-in-sugar option. These cakes get their sweet taste from the cornmeal.

2 cups boiling water
1 cup yellow cornmeal
1 Tbsp. sugar
1 tsp. salt
1½ cups milk
2 cups flour
1 Tbsp. baking powder
2 eggs

Makes 30 to 35 pancakes. Honey butter is a favorite with these.

In large bowl, blend together boiling water, cornmeal, sugar, and salt. Set aside for 5 minutes. Stir in milk and set aside for an additional 5 minutes.

In medium bowl, combine flour and baking powder. Beat eggs into the cornmeal mix; then beat in flour mixture until smooth.

Heat a large skillet or griddle over medium heat and brush with oil. Drop a heaping serving in prepared skillet and cook for 3 to 5 minutes or until bottom is golden brown and top is speckled with holes. Turn the pancake and brown the other side. Serve warm.

Blueberry Drizzle Pancakes

Just when you thought you couldn't get enough blueberry flavor, pour some warm
blueberry sauce over the top. Way too good!

1 cup flour
1 Tbsp. sugar
1½ tsp. baking powder
¼ tsp. cinnamon
¾ cup fresh blueberries
½ tsp. salt
1 egg
¾ cup milk
2 Tbsp. butter or margarine,
  melted

Preheat a large skillet or griddle over medium heat.

In large bowl, blend together the flour, sugar, baking powder, cinnamon, blueberries, and salt.

In medium bowl, beat egg until foamy. Beat in milk and butter. Combine the two mixtures, stirring until the ingredients are combined but the batter is still slightly lumpy.

Brush skillet with oil. Drop a heaping serving in prepared skillet and cook for 3 to 5 minutes or until bottom is golden brown and top is speckled with holes. Turn the pancake and brown the other side. Serve warm with Quick Warm Blueberry Sauce (see page 131).

Oat Bran Pancakes

A great healthy choice bursting with flavor. They taste so good! These pancakes are golden brown on the outside and light and fluffy inside.

½ cup flour
¾ cup oat bran
2 tsp. sugar
2 tsp. baking powder
¼ tsp. ground nutmeg
¼ tsp. salt
1 egg
¾ cup whole milk
1 Tbsp. butter, melted

Preheat a large skillet or griddle over medium heat.

In large bowl, blend together flour, oat bran, sugar, baking powder, nutmeg, and salt.

In medium bowl, beat the egg until foamy. Beat in milk and butter. Combine the two mixtures, beating until smooth.

Brush the skillet with oil. Drop a heaping serving in prepared skillet and cook for 3 to 5 minutes or until bottom is golden brown and top is speckled with holes. Turn the pancake and brown the other side. Serve warm.

Sun-kissed Orange Pancakes

These pancakes have the refreshing taste of sun-kissed orange juice.
Try them with ham and eggs for a fantastic way to start the day.

1 egg
2 Tbsp. butter, melted
1 cup orange juice
1 cup flour
2 tsp. baking powder
1 Tbsp. sugar
½ tsp. salt

Preheat a large skillet over medium heat.

In blender, combine the egg, butter and orange juice. Process on high for about 20 seconds or until smooth. Add the flour, baking powder, sugar, and salt; process for an additional 20 seconds or until smooth.

Brush the skillet with oil. Drop a heaping serving in prepared skillet and cook for 3 to 5 minutes or until bottom is golden brown and top is speckled with holes. Turn the pancake and brown the other side. Serve warm.

Smooth Cream Cheese Pancakes

The combination of cream cheese, sour cream, and butter makes these pancakes rich and smooth to the taste. They are so good that even the drowsiest people have a reason to get out of bed in the morning.

3 Tbsp. flour
2 Tbsp. sugar
¼ tsp. salt
9 oz. (3 small pkgs.) cream
   cheese
3 Tbsp. sour cream
¼ cup butter, melted
3 eggs

Preheat a large skillet over medium heat.

In small bowl, combine flour, sugar, and salt.

In large bowl, beat cream cheese until soft before beating in sour cream and butter. Add eggs, one at a time, beating well after each addition. Combine the two mixtures, beating until smooth.

Brush the skillet with oil. Drop a heaping serving in prepared skillet and cook for 3 to 5 minutes or until bottom is golden brown and top is speckled with holes. Turn the pancake and brown the other side. Serve warm. Makes 4 to 6 servings.

Berry du Jour

The wild blackberry is very tart. The cultivated varieties tend to be less so.
Sunday brunch or any special occasion is perfect for this wonderful fruit pastry.

Pancake:

3 Tbsp. margarine, melted,
   divided
1 cup milk
6 eggs
1 cup flour
½ tsp. salt
2 Tbsp. powdered sugar

Berry Topping:

3 cups (any combination)
   raspberries,
 blueberries, blackberries, sliced
   strawberries
⅓ cup orange marmalade

Preheat oven to 450°F.

Topping, gently stir together berries and marmalade in medium size bowl. Set aside.

Pancake: Grease a round glass pie plate. In medium size bowl, combine milk, eggs, and remaining 2 tablespoons margarine using a whisk. Slowly whisk in combined flour and salt until egg mixture is smooth. Pour batter into pie plate.

Bake 13 minutes. Reduce oven temperature to 350°F and continue baking 15 to 17 minutes or until sides are crisp and golden brown. Remove pancake from the oven and immediately dust with powdered sugar. Fill the center with berry topping and cut into wedges; serve warm.

Kids' Choice Award

Savor the wonderful aroma of home-baked cookies for breakfast. This is a family pleaser with plump raisins and hearty oatmeal. Definitely a delicious way to start the day.

⅓ cup flour
2 cups rolled oats
2 tsp. sugar
2½ tsp. baking powder
1 tsp. salt
2 eggs, separated
2 cups milk
1 Tbsp. butter, melted
½ cup raisins
chocolate chips (optional)

Preheat a large skillet or griddle over medium heat.

In large bowl, blend together flour, rolled oats, sugar, baking powder, and salt.

In small bowl, beat the egg whites until stiff but not dry.

In medium bowl, beat egg yolks, milk, and butter together. Combine oat and milk mixtures, beating until smooth. Fold in egg whites; add raisins.

Brush the skillet with oil. Drop a heaping serving in prepared skillet and cook for 3 to 5 minutes or until bottom is golden brown and top is speckled with holes. Turn the pancake and brown the other side. Serve warm.

Swedish Pancakes

Not only are these fancy looking, but they are rich and so easy! Topping choices are endless.
Fruit and whipped cream are easy favorites.

2¼ cups flour
1½ tsp. sugar
¾ tsp. salt
¾ tsp. baking powder
3 cups whole milk
3 Tbsp. butter, melted
3 eggs, beaten
1½ tsp. vanilla

In large bowl, mix flour, sugar, salt, and baking powder. Stir in remaining ingredients; beat with hand-held wire whisk until smooth. Batter will be thin.

Lightly butter 8-inch skillet. Over medium heat, rotate pan in a swirling motion to coat pan completely and heat butter until bubbly. Pour in ¼ cup batter and swirl in pan. Cook until light browned. Turn over and cook other side.

Remove immediately and place on plate. Fill center with desired filling and roll pancake up from one end. Add more toppings to top if desired.

Pioneer Sourdough

I'll bet your Grandmas made a version of these griddle cakes. Sit back and enjoy the simple comfort flavor of this old-time favorite.

2 cups flour
½ tsp. baking soda
2 Tbsp. sugar
2 cups sour milk
1 Tbsp. vegetable shortening, melted
1 egg, beaten

Stir all dry ingredients together. Add milk, melted vegetable shortening, and beaten egg; stir.

Drop batter by spoonfuls onto hot, greased griddle. Cook until light brown; turn over to brown other side.

Serve hot with maple syrup. Makes approximately 18 cakes.

Golden Penny Pancakes

*This is the cousin to the Silver Dollar Pancake. Just one look at these pancakes
and you can easily see where they get their name.*

1 cup and 2 Tbsp. flour
2¼ tsp. sugar
2¼ tsp. baking powder
1½ cup sharp cheddar cheese,
   shredded
1½ cups milk
1 egg
3 tsp. vegetable oil

Mix together flour, sugar, baking powder,
and cheese. In separate bowl, beat milk,
egg, and oil. Stir egg mixture into flour
mixture until just combined.

Heat a lightly oiled skillet over medium
heat. Using a measuring cup, pour ½ cup
batter onto the skillet. Brown on both
sides. Serve hot.

Good with maple syrup, fruit, or nothing
at all.

Applesauce Pancakes

You'll enjoy these easy-to-make pancakes. Serve with extra warm applesauce to pour over the top. Let these be the "apple" of your eye!

1 cup flour
1 tsp. baking soda
$\frac{1}{8}$ tsp. salt
2 Tbsp. toasted wheat germ
1 cup nonfat buttermilk
$\frac{1}{4}$ cup applesauce
2 tsp. vegetable oil
1 egg, lightly beaten
reduced-calorie maple syrup
    (optional)
fresh fruit slices (optional)

Combine first 4 ingredients in medium bowl; make a well in center of mixture.

Combine buttermilk and next 3 ingredients. Add buttermilk mixture to dry ingredients, stirring just until dry ingredients are moistened.

Grease a nonstick griddle or nonstick skillet and preheat to 350°F.

For each pancake, pour $\frac{1}{4}$ cup batter onto hot griddle, spreading to a 5-inch circle. Cook pancakes until tops are covered with bubbles and edges look cooked; turn pancakes and cook other side. If desired, serve with maple syrup and fresh fruit slices. Makes 10 (5-inch) pancakes.

Banana Cinnamon Pancakes

The butter and olive oil mixture added to the skillet makes for a nice subtle flavor and crispiness around the edges when cooked.

1 cup flour
1 tsp. cinnamon
2 tsp. sugar
1 cup milk
1 egg, large
1 tsp. vanilla
1 banana, mashed
butter
olive oil
maple syrup

In medium bowl, sift flour, cinnamon, and sugar together. Add milk, egg, vanilla, and banana to dry ingredients. Mix with a whisk until well combined.

Combine equal parts of butter and olive oil. Heat skillet and grease with butter and oil mixture.

Pour ¾ cup batter into hot skillet; wait until bubbles form on top of pancakes. When they burst, flip pancake. Cook until golden brown. Top with butter and maple syrup. Makes 12 pancakes.

French Toast

French Toast

So, what defines French toast recipes? The first thing to know is that French toast isn't really French at all! The first piece of bread soaked in egg batter and cooked seems to have originated in Rome. Today, just about every country around the globe has their own version of this classic breakfast food. And by the way, don't look for "French toast" on any menu in France because the French refer to it as "pain perdu."

French toast is a great way to make use of all the dry or day-old bread you can't bear to throw away. Older bread is actually better for French toast, as it absorbs the egg better without falling apart.

Most recipes can be more versatile when it comes to the type of bread you use: sourdough, wheat, white, French, potato, cinnamon raisin, or multi grains. The choice is up to you. Different breads can enhance the flavor and nutritional value of your recipe. When using thin slices of bread, serve them cut at a diagonal.

Apple Cinnamon French Toast

Cinnamon and apples together are a natural combination—each one complements the other.
Extra moist and extra chewy, a delicious way to make French toast!

2 eggs
¾ cup milk
2 Tbsp. sugar
1 tsp. cinnamon
¼ cup applesauce
6 slices of bread

In large mixing bowl, combine the eggs, milk, sugar, cinnamon, and applesauce; mix well.

Soak bread, one slice at a time, until saturated with liquid.

Cook on a lightly greased griddle over medium-high heat until lightly browned on both sides. Serve hot.

Fast and Furious French Toast

This recipe is such a time saver. Pop the French toast into the oven and let it bake.
You'll be glad you won't have to spend time standing in front of the stove.

French Toast:

1 loaf French bread, sliced
6 eggs
1½ cups skim milk
1 Tbsp. vanilla
⅓ cup sugar
6 apples, cored, peeled, and
  sliced
2 Tbsp. sugar
1½ tsp. cinnamon
½ tsp. ground nutmeg

Topping:

¼ cup flour
½ sugar
½ cup margarine, melted
½ cup brown sugar
½ cup milk
2 tsp. vanilla

Lightly grease a 9x13-inch baking pan. If possible use glass; it will help prevent toast from sticking.

French Toast: Cut bread into 1½-inch thick slices and place in pan.

In large bowl, beat eggs with milk, sugar, and vanilla. Pour egg mixture over bread slices.

Arrange apples slices on top of bread. Sprinkle cinnamon, nutmeg, and 2 tablespoons sugar over apples.

Cover pan and refrigerate overnight.

In the morning, preheat oven to 350°F. Bake bread mixture about 1 hour until golden brown.

Topping: Make topping while French toast is baking. Combine the flour, white sugar, and margarine. Stir in brown sugar, milk, and vanilla. Pour mixture into a small saucepan. Cook on low until thick. Serve French toast warm with caramel sauce.

Banana Bread French Toast

You'll be pleasantly surprised at this moist and delicious new way to enjoy banana bread.

....

3 eggs
3 Tbsp. sweetened condensed
   milk
1 tsp. vanilla
2 Tbsp. butter
1 loaf banana bread
powdered sugar

In shallow bowl, whisk together eggs, sweetened condensed milk, and vanilla with a fork. Set aside.

Melt butter in large skillet over medium heat. Slice banana bread into 4 thick slices. Dip each slice into the egg mixture; then place in the hot skillet. Cook on each side until golden brown.

Dust with powdered sugar. Serve warm. Great with whipped butter or cream.

Speckled Egg Bread

This recipe is so different and delicious!
Great for holidays or company. It's easy to prepare the night before and bake in the morning.

French Toast:
1 loaf French bread, cut into 1-
   inch cubes
1 (8 oz.) cream cheese, diced
1 cup blueberries
2 cups milk
12 eggs
⅓ cup maple syrup

Sauce:
1 cup sugar
2 Tbsp. cornstarch
1 cup water
1 cup blueberries
1 Tbsp. butter

French Toast: Place half of the bread cubes in lightly greased, 9x13-inch baking pan. Sprinkle cream cheese cubes on top of bread cubes. Top with 1 cup blueberries and remaining bread.

In large bowl, beat together milk, eggs, and maple syrup. Pour egg mixture over bread. Cover pan and refrigerate overnight.

The next morning, remove pan from refrigerator 30 minutes before baking. Preheat oven to 350°F.

Cover pan with aluminum foil and bake in preheated oven for 30 minutes. Uncover and bake an additional 30 minutes or until golden brown and center is set.

Sauce: In saucepan, combine sugar and cornstarch; add water. Boil over medium heat for 3 minutes, stirring constantly. Stir in blueberries and reduce heat.

Simmer 8 to 10 minutes, or until the berries have burst. Stir in butter until melted.

Cut French toast into squares to serve. Pour the sauce over the squares. Serve warm.

Cinnamon Swirl French Toast

Using cinnamon swirl bread makes this especially great for cinnamon toast lovers.
My family likes the kind that has a frosting glaze on top.

3 eggs
½ cup milk
½ tsp. cinnamon
1 Tbsp. plus 1 tsp. margarine,
　divided
4 slices cinnamon swirl bread

Combine first 3 ingredients in shallow bowl, stirring well with a wire whisk.

Grease a nonstick skillet. Add 1 teaspoon margarine; place pan over medium heat until margarine melts. Dip 1 bread slice into egg mixture. Place coated bread in skillet; cook until browned and crisp on each side, turning once. Repeat with remaining slices. Makes 4 servings.

Crispy French Toast

*Don't knock it until you've tried it. The cornflakes add a nice crunchy coating.
My kids really enjoy this wacky version of French toast.*

8 cups vegetable oil
   for deep-frying
6 thick slices white bread
2 eggs
1 cup milk
1 tsp. vanilla
1 tsp. cinnamon
1 Tbsp. sugar
2 cups cornflakes cereal

Preheat deep-fryer to 375°F.

In large bowl, combine eggs, milk, vanilla, cinnamon, and sugar; beat well. Place corn-flakes in separate bowl.

Dip bread slices in egg mixture and press into cornflakes.

Carefully slide coated bread slices into hot oil. Fry on each side until golden brown. Drain on paper towels and serve hot.

English Muffin French Toast

Use cinnamon raisin English muffins or any type you like. The air holes help speed up the cooking time. I am really impressed with these. They look like English Crumpets when cooked.

2 eggs
½ cup milk
½ tsp. ground nutmeg
¼ tsp. salt
6 cinnamon raisin English
   muffins, cut in half
2 Tbsp. butter
1 cup sugar

Mix eggs, milk, nutmeg, and salt together with a fork until well mixed. Pour mixture into a low, flat pan or a large, shallow dish.

Let the halves soak on each side in the egg mixture.

Heat a griddle over medium heat. Put about a ½ tablespoon of butter in the pan and let it melt. Place muffin halves in the pan. Cook for 2 to 3 minutes on each side.

Spread a layer of sugar on a plate and dip both sides of muffin in sugar just before serving. Serve warm.

Serve plain or with warm maple syrup.

Cinnamon Roll French Toast

Cream cheese frosting makes this French toast just incredible!
For a low fat version use fat-free cream cheese and sour cream.

French Toast:

6 eggs

1½ cups milk

2 tsp. cinnamon

2 Tbsp. sugar

1 loaf French bread, cut into 1-
inch slices

¼ cup butter

Frosting:

1 (8 oz.) pkg. cream cheese,
softened

2 Tbsp. sour cream

2 Tbsp. sugar

2 Tbsp. whipped topping

French Toast: In medium bowl, whisk together the eggs, milk, cinnamon, and sugar.

Melt 1 tablespoon of butter in a large griddle over medium heat. Dip bread slices into egg mixture just to coat. Place in the hot griddle, and cook until golden brown on both sides, about 4 minutes each side. Repeat with each piece of bread. Keep griddle well greased with butter throughout cooking.

While toast is cooking, mix cream cheese, sour cream, sugar, and whipped topping with an electric mixer until smooth and firm.

Serve warm with sour cream frosting.

Hawaiian French Toast

Indulge yourself and sprinkle on coconut and chopped macadamia nuts.
You'll think you're in Paradise.

3 eggs
½ tsp. vanilla
1 Tbsp. honey
1 Tbsp. water
1 tsp. grated orange peel
1 loaf Hawaiian sweet bread,
  sliced thick
1 (8 oz.) can pineapple, crushed,
  with juice
1 (3 oz.) can mandarin oranges
1 cup maple syrup
3 Tbsp. honey

In shallow bowl, whisk together eggs, vanilla, honey, water, and orange peel.

Coat bread slices in egg mixture; set aside.

In small saucepan, combine crushed pineapple, mandarin oranges, maple syrup, and honey. Simmer over low heat for 4 minutes.

Heat a lightly oiled griddle over medium high heat.

Fry bread slices until brown on both sides. Serve hot with warm fruit sauce.

Sprinkle with coconut and chopped macadamia nuts.

Just Peachy French Toast

Great to share with the girls.
Just be sure to have plenty of whipped topping to smother on top.

½ cup butter
1 cup brown sugar, packed
2 Tbsp. water
1 (29 oz.) can sliced peaches,
   drained
12 slices day-old French bread
   (3-inch thick slices)
5 eggs
1 Tbsp. vanilla
¼ tsp. cinnamon

In saucepan, stir together the butter, brown sugar, and water. Bring to a boil; then reduce heat to low, simmer 10 minutes, stirring frequently.

Pour the brown sugar mixture into a 9x13-inch baking dish, covering the bottom of the pan completely. Place peaches in a layer over the sugar coating. Place French bread slices over sugar mixture.

In medium bowl, whisk together the eggs and vanilla. Pour evenly over the bread slices to coat. Sprinkle cinnamon over the top.

Cover and refrigerate 8 hours or overnight.

Remove from refrigerator before baking and bring to room temperature. Uncover.

Preheat oven to 350°F; bake 30 minutes or until the bread is golden brown. Spoon out portions to serve. Serve with plenty of whipped topping.

Raspberry Cheesecake-Filled French Toast

French toast will never be the same! Now you're taking it to new heights. Rather easy, yet seems so fancy with its creamy filling. You'll definitely make this French toast more often.

1 cup milk
2 Tbsp. vanilla
2 Tbsp. cinnamon
1 cup sugar
4 eggs, beaten
1 cup raspberry jam
4 oz. cream cheese, softened
1 loaf French bread, cut into 1-
   inch slices
butter
powdered sugar

In bowl, whisk milk, vanilla, cinnamon, and sugar into the beaten eggs until well blended. Set aside.

In separate bowl, cream together raspberry jam and cream cheese until smooth.

Cut each slice of bread in half and spread raspberry cream cheese mixture in the center of each slice, making a sandwich.

Melt butter over medium heat in a large skillet or griddle. Dip bread into egg mixture, coating thoroughly.

Cook until well-browned on both sides, about 5 minutes.

Dust with powdered sugar. Serve immediately. Makes 8 servings.

Cinnamon Cream French Toast

The cinnamon cream syrup is an extra bonus.

Note: the secret that makes these fluffy is the addition of flour.

French Toast:
¼ cup flour
1 cup milk
pinch of salt
3 eggs
1 tsp. vanilla
1 Tbsp. sugar
½ tsp. cinnamon
12 thick slices French bread

Cinnamon Cream Syrup:
1 cup sugar
½ cup corn syrup
¼ cup water
1 (5 oz.) can evaporated milk
1 tsp. vanilla extract
½ tsp. cinnamon

French Toast: In large bowl, add flour; slowly whisk in the milk. Whisk in salt, eggs, vanilla, sugar, and cinnamon until smooth.

Heat a lightly oiled griddle over medium heat.

Soak bread slices in mixture until saturated. Cook bread on each side until golden brown.

Meanwhile, for the syrup, combine the sugar, corn syrup, and water in a small saucepan. Bring to a boil over medium heat; cook and stir 2 minutes or until thickened. Remove from heat; stir in the evaporated milk, vanilla, and cinnamon. Serve over warm French toast.

French Toast Almondine

This is a nice twist to the traditional French toast. The toasted almonds add a nice, nutty flavor.
Serve with fresh fruit or yogurt.

1 cup slivered almonds
3 eggs
1 cup milk
3 Tbsp. flour
½ tsp. baking powder
¼ tsp. salt
½ tsp. almond extract
1 tsp. vanilla
12 thick slices French bread
4 Tbsp. oil
4 Tbsp. butter
powdered sugar

Place almonds in a small saucepan over low heat.

Tossing frequently, toast until lightly browned, 5 to 10 minutes. Remove from heat and set aside.

In large bowl, whisk together eggs, milk, flour, baking powder, salt, almond extract, and vanilla. Soak bread slices in mixture until saturated. Place slices in a shallow pan. Refrigerate slices approximately 1 hour.

Heat oil and butter in a large skillet over medium heat. One at a time, press one side of soaked bread slices in almonds to coat. Fry bread slices on both sides until golden brown.

French Toast 'Le Chocolat'

Any chocolate lover would appreciate this beauty! Great for breakfast or as a dessert.
Whipped cream cuddles up nicely to this toast.

....

3 eggs
¾ cup milk
2 Tbsp. cocoa powder
2 Tbsp. sugar
¼ tsp. vanilla extract
⅛ tsp. salt
½ tsp. cinnamon
8–10 bread slices, thickly sliced
powdered sugar
whipped cream

Heat griddle over medium heat. Grease griddle with margarine or cooking spray.

In medium bowl, beat eggs, milk, cocoa powder, sugar, vanilla, salt, and cinnamon until smooth.

Dip bread in egg mixture. Place on griddle—do not let pieces touch. Cook about 4 minutes on each side.

Serve immediately with powdered sugar or pancake syrup, if desired.

Garnish with whipped cream. Makes 8 to 10 pieces of French toast.

Waffles

Waffles

Waffles seem to be viewed as a luxury. To order a waffle in a restaurant is like really splurging on something new. I know they can seem time consuming and slow to make since they are baked one at a time.

We had a waffle family tradition as a kid. Christmas morning after the gifts were opened we would have waffles. Whipped cream and strawberries were a must. Bacon and eggs and plenty of butter and maple syrup were always available. Then as we grew up and left home, starting families of our own, we moved the waffle tradition to Christmas Eve. This left time for us to spend Christmas mornings at our homes with our children, leaving plenty of time to spend at Grandma's for Christmas dinner.

Waffles are some of the oldest breakfast foods around. Ancient Greeks made flat cakes between two metal plates. The word waffle actually comes from a Dutch word, "wafel," and this is probably the origin of the food as we know it.

They first became popular in England as a dessert item, commonly served topped with ice cream, custard yogurts, and whipped cream. A garnish of fruit or fruit topped it off. Americans adopted the waffle as a breakfast item. My theory of eating dessert first comes true again. Waffles used to be street food, too. Vendors sold them steaming hot and dripping with maple syrup or molasses.

Waffles are especially great for leftovers with no waste. If you find you have batter mix remaining, cook all the batter and package and freeze individually. They can be dropped into the toaster for a quick breakfast.

Waffle irons now come in such fun shapes and sizes. I suggest owning more than one. Thrift stores and garage sales are an inexpensive way to collect extras to keep costs down and production fast. Nowadays, the professional restaurant-style waffle irons are also available. The Professional Belgian Waffle Maker produces a large, restaurant-style waffle with extra deep squares to hold fruit and syrup.

A good waffle iron is a necessary tool of the trade because they use high heat that cooks quickly and crisps the outside of the waffle while leaving the inside tender and light. It is the 180° rotary feature that ensures consistent baking and even browning on both sides.

Or do what I do; place a hot pad under the waffle iron. I start with the waffle iron placed upside down. Always remember to spray the top and bottom of the iron well between each waffle before pouring in the batter. Open and pour in waffle batter on the upside-down waffle iron. Be sure to use caution—the irons are very hot! Then after the batter is in, close the top (which is really the bottom) and wait a few seconds for the batter to distribute evenly. Then flip the waffle iron back over to its right side to continue the baking process. Professional results without professional waffle iron prices!

So if you love restaurant style (or any other style) waffles, now you can have them at home. Remember, they aren't just for breakfast anymore. With all the shapes available, just have fun and enjoy!

● Waffle Tips

When making waffles or pancakes, be sure and mix the batter between batches to avoid settling. You will be surprised at the difference in quality.

Apple Orchard Waffles

The traditional flavor duo of apples and cinnamon combines into the aroma of baked apples.

Note: Substitute a grated apple or applesauce for the chopped apple if a smoother texture is desired.

1½ cups flour
1 tsp. sugar
1 Tbsp. baking powder
¾ cup chopped apple
¼ tsp. salt
¼ tsp. cinnamon
2 eggs
1 cup milk
¼ Tbsp. butter, melted

Preheat a waffle iron and oil as required.

In large bowl, whisk together the flour, sugar, baking powder, apple, salt, and cinnamon. In small bowl, using an electric mixer on medium speed, beat the eggs until foamy. Beat in milk and butter. Combine the two mixtures, blending until the dry ingredients are well moistened and the batter is smooth.

Pour ½ cup of the batter onto waffle iron and bake according to the manufacturer's instructions. Remove waffle from iron and repeat until all the batter is used. Serve hot with a sprinkling of cinnamon sugar.

Bacon Waffles

When I tell my family we are having bacon waffles, they say, "what time?"

1½ cups flour
½ cup graham flour
1 Tbsp. baking powder
1 Tbsp. sugar
½ cup crispy cooked bacon,
   crumbled
¼ tsp. salt
2 eggs
2 cups milk
½ cup warmed bacon drippings

Preheat waffle iron and oil.

In large bowl, whisk together the two flours, baking powder, sugar, bacon, and salt.

In medium bowl, using a whisk, beat eggs until foamy. Beat in milk and bacon drippings. Combine the two mixtures, blending until dry ingredients are moistened and batter is smooth.

Pour ½ cup of the batter into the center of the waffle iron and bake according to the manufacturer's directions. Remove the waffles and continue until all the batter is used. Serve hot with whipped butter and maple syrup on the side.

Banana Boat Waffles

Have some fun with this one. Let your kids spread peanut butter all over these.
Top with more sliced bananas.

2 cups flour
1 Tbsp. sugar
2¼ tsp. baking powder
¾ tsp. salt
3 eggs, separated
1½ cups milk
½ cup vegetable shortening,
    melted
1 cup banana, mashed

Preheat waffle iron and oil.

In large bowl, combine the flour, sugar, baking powder, and salt. In small bowl, using an electric mixer on high speed, beat the egg whites until stiff but not dry.

In medium bowl, using an electric mixer on medium speed, beat egg yolks until thick and light-colored.

Beat in milk, shortening, and bananas. Combine dry ingredients with the egg yolk mixture, blending until the dry ingredients are moistened and the batter is smooth. Fold in egg whites.

Pour ½ cup of the batter into center of waffle iron and bake according to the manufacturer's directions.

Remove the waffle and continue until all the batter is used. Serve hot. Makes 6 waffles.

Belgian Waffles

These are Brussels-style waffles sure to please anyone!

2 cups flour
2 tsp. baking powder
2 Tbsp. powdered sugar
1 Tbsp. vegetable oil
2 cups milk
3 eggs, separated
2 tsp. vanilla
pinch of salt
fruit of your choice
whipped cream

Combine the flour, baking powder, powdered sugar, oil, milk, and egg yolks. Beat egg whites until they stand in soft peaks; then fold into the batter—do not over mix.

Using a ladle, pour $\frac{1}{8}$ of mixture into a greased, hot waffle iron and bake for about 2 minutes. Repeat with remaining batter. Top with the fruit and whipped cream; serve hot. Makes 8 waffles.

Blueberry Pleasure

These waffles are a Northwest signature.

2 cups flour
4 tsp. baking powder
¼ tsp. ground nutmeg
½ tsp. salt
2 eggs
½ cup margarine, melted
1¾ cups heavy cream
2 Tbsp. sugar
½ cup fresh or frozen
　blueberries, thawed and
　drained

Preheat waffle iron and oil.

In large bowl, combine the flour, baking powder, nutmeg, and salt. In medium bowl, using an electric mixer, beat the eggs until foamy. Beat in margarine. In medium bowl, using an electric mixer on high speed, beat the cream and sugar together until a soft peak forms. Fold in blueberries. Combine egg and cream mixtures, blending until smooth. Stir in dry ingredients, blending until dry ingredients are moistened and batter is smooth.

Pour ½ cup of the batter into center of the waffle iron and bake according to the manufacturer's directions.

Remove the waffle and continue until all the batter is used. Serve hot.

Buttermilk Pecan Waffles

This is one to pass on through the generations.

....

2 cups flour
1 Tbsp. baking soda
1 Tbsp. baking powder
½ tsp. salt
4 eggs
2 cups buttermilk
½ cup butter or margarine
3 Tbsp. chopped pecans

Combine flour, baking soda, baking powder, and salt; set aside.

In mixing bowl, beat eggs until light. Add buttermilk; mix well. Add dry ingredients and beat until batter is smooth. Stir in butter. Pour about ¾ cup batter onto a lightly greased, preheated waffle iron. Sprinkle with a few pecans. Bake according to manufacturer's directions until golden brown. Repeat until batter and pecans are gone. Makes 7 waffles.

Cornflake Waffles

Miss your morning cereal? Here's a way to have it all!

....

1¼ cup flour
2 Tbsp. sugar
2¼ tsp. baking powder
1 cup cornflakes
½ tsp. salt
3 eggs, separated
1 cup milk
¼ cup shortening, melted

Preheat waffle iron and oil.

In large bowl, combine flour, sugar, baking powder, cornflakes, and salt. In medium bowl, using electric mixer on medium speed, beat the egg yolk, milk, and shortening until smooth. In small bowl, using an electric mixer on high speed, beat the egg whites until stiff but not dry. Combine all dry ingredients and egg yolk mixture, blending until the dry ingredients are moistened and the batter is smooth. Fold in egg whites.

Pour ½ cup of the batter into center of waffle iron and bake according to the manufacturer's directions.

Remove the waffle and continue until all the batter is used.

Serve hot with whipped fruit butter and syrup of choice.

Idaho Potato Waffles

If you like the texture of potato bread, you will surely like the moist texture of this waffle.
Top with plenty of whipped butter and maple syrup.

Note: Instant potatoes will work great for this recipe.

1 cup flour
2 tsp. baking powder
½ tsp. ground nutmeg
½ tsp. salt
3 eggs
1 Tbsp. butter or margarine, melted
1 cup milk
2 cups mashed potatoes

Preheat waffle iron and oil.

In large bowl, combine flour, baking powder, nutmeg, and salt. In medium bowl, using an electric mixer on medium speed, beat the eggs until thick and light-colored. Beat in butter, milk, and potatoes. Combine the two mixtures, blending until the dry ingredients are moistened and the batter is smooth.

Pour ½ cup of the batter into center of waffle iron and bake according to the manufacturer's directions.

Remove the waffle and continue until all the batter is used.

Serve hot with whipped butter and maple syrup.

Country Inn Waffles

Delicious with fresh fruit, yogurt, and whipped cream.
Have fun! Homemade taste at its best.

1 cup sifted cake flour
1 tsp. baking soda
1 tsp. baking powder
1 tsp. sugar
$\frac{1}{8}$ tsp. salt
3 egg yolks
2 cups thick sour cream
3 egg whites

Sift together flour, baking soda, baking powder, sugar, and salt. In separate bowl, beat egg yolks until light; add sour cream. Combine with dry ingredients. Beat egg whites until stiff but not dry; fold into batter. Grease waffle iron. Bake in hot waffle iron.

Grains Galore

Serve with the warm pear-honey butter and you'll know why they call breakfast the meal that sets the tone of the day. What a great start!

Waffle:
1 cup flour
1 cup whole-wheat flour
1 Tbsp. baking powder
1 tsp. salt
2 large eggs
½ cup butter or margarine, melted
1¼ cups milk

Pear-Honey Butter:
1 (16 oz.) can pear halves
2 Tbsp. honey

Preheat waffle iron and oil.

Waffle: In large bowl, combine the two flours, baking powder, and salt. In medium bowl, beat eggs until thick and light-colored. Beat in margarine and milk. Combine the two mixtures, blending until dry ingredients are moistened and batter is smooth.

Pour ½ cup of the batter into center of waffle iron and bake according to the manufacturer's directions.

Remove the waffle and continue until all the batter is gone. Serve hot. Try with warm honey and powdered sugar or pear-honey butter.

Pear-Honey Butter: Drain pears; mash pears to the consistency of chunky applesauce using a potato masher or pastry blender. Stir in honey. Serve warm or cold.

Muffins

Muffins

Muffins are great for any meal, from a quick breakfast-on-the-run to an elegant brunch. Everyone loves muffins. Simple to make and delicious to eat. There are sweet and savory muffins for every taste.

● Muffin Tips

The key to great muffins is to combine liquid and dry ingredients just until dry ingredients are moistened; some lumps will remain.

For rounded tops on muffins, grease only the bottom of the cup and halfway up the side.

If muffin cups are filled more than two-thirds full, the muffins will have flat, "flying saucer" tops. If sufficient room is not allowed for muffins to expand before reaching the top of the cup the muffin will flatten on top.

Bake as soon as the batter is mixed. When filling cups, do not mix batter between scoops. Excessive mixing causes loss of leavening.

Paper liners keep muffins fresh longer. They peel off easier on muffins served at room temperature rather than warm from the oven.

Flaky Apple Muffins

This muffin, served with yogurt and fruit or a wedge of soft cheese, makes breakfast a special occasion.

1 cup flour
⅓ cup packed brown sugar
2 tsp. baking powder
½ tsp. salt
½ tsp. cinnamon
¼ tsp. ground nutmeg
1 cup (1 medium) tart apple,
    peeled and finely chopped
¾ cup water
½ cup dry milk
¼ cup vegetable oil
1 large egg
2 cups bran flake cereal

Preheat oven to 400°F. Grease or paper line 12 muffin cups.

Combine flour, brown sugar, baking powder, salt, cinnamon, and nutmeg in medium bowl. Mix apple, water, dry milk, vegetable oil, and egg in small bowl; add to flour mixture and stir until moistened. Stir in bran flake cereal. Spoon batter ⅔ full into greased muffin cups.

Bake for 13 to 15 minutes. Remove to wire rack; serve warm.

Blueberry Buttermilk Muffins

Bursting with berries, these are the best blueberry muffins of all.
An extra half cup of blueberries mashed is the secret.

....

2½ cups flour
1 cup sugar
2½ tsp. baking powder
¼ tsp. salt
1 cup buttermilk
2 eggs, beaten
½ cup butter, melted
1½ cups fresh or frozen
    blueberries (mash ½ cup with
    a fork)

Preheat oven to 400°F F. Stir together flour, sugar, baking powder, and salt in a large mixing bowl. Combine buttermilk, eggs, and butter; blend well. Add to flour mixture; stir just until dry ingredients are moistened. Fold in blueberries.

Spoon into buttered 2½ inch muffin cups, filling three-fourths full. Bake 20 minutes or until golden brown.

Cool in muffin pan on a wire rack 5 minutes. Remove from pan. Serve warm.

Chocolate Streusel Pecan Muffins

These streusel muffins have chocolate chips in them. The buttery pecan streusel topping makes these a crowd pleaser. Enjoy for breakfast or as a snack anytime.

Topping:
¼ cup flour
¼ cup brown sugar, packed
¼ tsp. cinnamon
2 Tbsp. butter, melted
¼ cup chopped pecans

Muffin:
1¾ cups chocolate chips
⅓ cup milk
3 Tbsp. butter
1 cup flour
2 Tbsp. sugar
2 tsp. baking powder
¼ tsp. cinnamon
¾ cup chopped pecans
1 large egg
½ tsp. vanilla

Topping: Combine flour, brown sugar, cinnamon, and butter with fork in small bowl until mixture resembles coarse crumbs. Stir in pecans.

Preheat oven to 375°F. Grease or paper line 12 muffin cups.

Muffins: Combine 1 cup chocolate chips, milk, and butter in a double boiler over hot water. Stir until morsels are melted and mixture is smooth.

In large bowl, combine flour, sugar, baking powder, cinnamon, pecans, and remaining ¾ cup chocolate chips.

In small bowl, combine egg, vanilla, and melted chocolate mixture. Stir into flour mixture just until moistened. Spoon into prepared muffins cups, filling ⅔ full.

Sprinkle with topping.

Bake for 20 to 25 minutes. Cool in pan for 5 minutes; remove from pan and place on wire rack. Cool completely.

Cinnamon-Oatmeal Muffins

*I have included oatmeal. This time it's okay. All mixed
together with apple and you have a friendly combination.*

1½ cups flour
1 Tbsp. baking powder
¼ tsp. salt
¾ cup quick-cooking oats,
   uncooked
⅔ cup brown sugar
¾ tsp. cinnamon
¾ cup skim milk
⅓ cup unsweetened
   applesauce
1½ tsp. vegetable oil
3 egg whites

Combine first six ingredients in a medium
bowl; make a well in center of mixture.

Combine milk, applesauce, oil, and egg
whites; add to dry ingredients, stirring just
until dry ingredients are moistened.

Spoon batter into 12 greased muffin pan
cups, filling each ¾ full. Bake at 400°F for
18 to 20 minutes or until golden. Remove
from pan immediately. Makes 1 dozen.

Raspberry-Lemon Muffins

Sweet and tart all in one.
The streusel topping adds great texture and is an added bonus.

Muffin:
1 (8 oz.) container lemon yogurt
½ cup oil
1 tsp. lemon peel
2 eggs
2 cups flour
½ cup sugar
2 tsp. baking powder
½ tsp. baking soda
1 cup raspberries

Topping:
⅓ cup sugar
¼ cup flour
2 Tbsp. margarine

Muffin: Combine lemon yogurt, oil, lemon peel, and eggs. Mix until well blended.

Combine flour, sugar, baking powder, and baking soda; mix. Combine with yogurt mixture—do not over mix. Gently fold in raspberries. Grease muffin tin. Fill cups ½ full.

Topping: Combine sugar, flour, and margarine. Mix until crumbly. Sprinkle on top.

Bake at 400°F for 11 to 13 minutes

Lemon-glazed Blueberry Muffins

A sweet-tart lemon glaze plus the blueberries make these muffins extra special.
Your friends will think you are showing off. (Why not?)

Muffin:

2 cups flour
½ cup sugar
1 tsp. baking powder
½ tsp. baking soda
½ tsp. salt
⅛ tsp. ground nutmeg
¼ cup butter
1¼ cups buttermilk
1 large egg
1 T. grated lemon peel
1 cup blueberries

Glaze:

1 Tbsp. lemon juice
½ cup powdered sugar

Preheat oven to 400°F.

Muffin: Combine flour, sugar, baking powder, baking soda, salt, and nutmeg in a medium bowl. Cut in butter until mixture resembles coarse meal.

Combine buttermilk, egg, and lemon peel. Stir well with a whisk. Add to flour mixture; stir just until moist. Gently fold in blueberries.

Spoon batter into 12 greased muffin cups. Bake at 400°F for 20 minutes or until the muffins spring back when lightly touched.

Remove muffins from pans immediately and place on a wire rack. Cool.

Glaze: Combine lemon juice and powdered sugar in small bowl. Drizzle glaze evenly over cooled muffins. Makes 12 muffins.

Berry Lemon Muffins

Not only will you enjoy the combination of these flavors but also the compliments from your family. The marionberry, a Northwest favorite, adds a twist you'll surely enjoy.

Muffin:
1¾ cups flour
⅓ cup sugar
2½ tsp. baking powder
1 tsp. lemon peel
¾ tsp. salt
1 egg, beaten
¾ cup milk
⅓ cup cooking oil
¾ cup marionberries

Topping:
½ cup melted butter
⅓ cup sugar

Muffin: Stir together flour, sugar, baking powder, lemon peel, and salt. Make a well in center of mixture.

Combine egg, milk, and oil. Add egg mixture all at once to flour mixture. Stir just until moistened. Batter should be lumpy. Very gently fold in berries. Spoon batter into 12 greased muffin cups.

Bake at 400°F for 15 to 20 minutes or until light brown. Remove muffins from pans and dip tops of muffins into the melted butter and sprinkle with sugar.

Tip: Blackberries or loganberries may be substituted.

Picnic Berry Bites

*Enjoy summer's bounty with your choice of raspberries
or blueberries baked into these delicious buttermilk corn muffins.*

1 cup flour
1 cup yellow cornmeal
½ cup sugar
2 tsp. baking powder
1 tsp. baking soda
½ tsp. salt
1 cup buttermilk
¼ cup vegetable oil
2 tsp. vanilla extract
1 large egg
1¼ cups raspberries or 1½ cups
   blueberries

Preheat oven to 400°F. Grease twelve
2½ x 1¼ muffin cups.

In large bowl, mix flour, cornmeal, sugar,
baking powder, baking soda, and salt. In
small bowl, with wire whisk or fork, beat
buttermilk, vegetable oil, vanilla, and egg
until blended; stir into flour mixture just
until moistened (batter will be lumpy).
Carefully fold in berries.

Spoon batter into muffin cups. Bake
muffins 20 to 25 minutes or until toothpick inserted in center of muffin comes out
clean. Immediately remove muffins from
pans; serve warm or cool on wire rack.
Makes 12 muffins.

Cranberry Almond Muffins

Whole cranberries add the tart flavor to these muffins. Start a new tradition on Thanksgiving. Your guests will enjoy these. Make extra to go home with leftovers.

1½ cups flour
½ cup sugar
1 tsp. baking powder
¼ tsp. baking soda
¼ tsp. salt
2 large eggs
¼ cup butter, melted
½ cup sour cream
½ tsp. almond extract
¾ cup sliced almonds (divided)
½ cup whole-berry cranberry
   sauce

Preheat oven to 375°F. Line muffin-tin cups with paper baking cups.

Mix flour, sugar, baking powder, baking soda, and salt in a large bowl; set aside.

Break eggs into medium size bowl. Whisk in butter, sour cream, and almond extract. When mixed—do not over mix—stir in ½ cup almonds.

Add egg mixture to dry ingredients and fold in just until moistened. Spoon 2 tablespoons of batter into each baking cup; there will be 8 in all. Top with a level tablespoon of cranberry sauce, then with remaining batter. Sprinkle with remaining almonds.

Bake 30 to 35 minutes or until brown and springy to the touch. Let stand 20 minutes before removing muffins from cups. Makes 8 muffins.

Raspberry Creme Muffins

The tangy, creamy texture of the cream cheese and the sweet, plump raspberries are a marriage made in muffin heaven. Although raspberries are my favorites, blackberries will do nicely.

Muffin:
½ cup butter, room temperature
¾ cup sugar
2 eggs
2 tsp. vanilla
½ cup milk
2 cups flour
2 tsp. baking powder
¼ tsp. salt
1 cup fresh raspberries
1 oz. cream cheese

Topping:
2 Tbsp. sugar
½ tsp. ground nutmeg

Preheat oven to 375°F. Grease a 12-cup muffin tin; set aside.

In medium size bowl, beat butter and sugar on high speed, scraping down the sides of the bowl often, until light and fluffy. Add eggs, one at a time, again scraping down the sides of the bowl and mixing well after each addition. Add vanilla and milk and mix well.

Combine flour, baking powder, and salt in a large bowl.

Toss raspberries and cream cheese; pinch off in small bits and drop into the flour mixture. Using a large plastic spatula, gently fold the butter mixture into the flour mixture just until the batter comes together —do not over mix.

Divide batter among muffin cups, filling each about ¾ of the way full.

Topping: Combine sugar and nutmeg and sprinkle over the tops.

Bake until muffins are golden brown and slowly spring back when touched lightly in the center, 20 to 25 minutes. Let cool for about 5 minutes before removing from cups. Serve warm.

Raspberry Crumble Muffins

This pretty muffin placed with a ribbon at the Western Washington State Fair.
One bite and you will understand why.

Muffin:
2½ cups flour
1 cup sugar
2½ tsp. baking powder
¼ tsp. salt
¾ cup sour cream
¼ cup milk
2 eggs, beaten
½ cup butter, melted
1½ cups fresh or frozen
   raspberries

Crumb Topping:
⅓ cup flour
2 Tbsp. sugar
2 Tbsp. butter, softened

Preheat oven to 400°F.

Muffin: Stir together flour, sugar, baking powder, and salt in large mixing bowl.

Combine sour cream, milk, eggs, and butter; blend well. Add to flour mixture; stir just until dry ingredients are moistened—do not over mix. Fold in raspberries.

Topping: In small bowl, combine flour with sugar, and cut in butter to form crumbs.

Spoon batter into buttered 2½-inch muffin cups, filling ¾ of the way full. Top with crumb topping.

Bake 20 minutes or until golden brown. Cool in muffin pan on a wire rack 5 minutes. Remove from pan. Serve warm. Makes 12 muffins.

Hearty Breakfast Muffins

Start your day off with this complete muffin. Hearty and tasty, this recipe makes only six, so double and freeze some for a quick breakfast on the go.

¼ cup buttermilk
3 Tbsp. butter
1 tsp. vanilla
1 egg
½ cup flour
½ cup whole-wheat flour
⅓ cup sugar
1½ tsp. baking powder
¼ tsp. cinnamon
⅛ tsp. cloves
¼ cup carrot, shredded
¼ cup zucchini, shredded
¼ cup pineapple, crushed
¼ cup sunflower seeds
2 Tbsp. coconut

Preheat oven to 400°F.

In large bowl, beat buttermilk, butter, vanilla, and egg. Stir in flour, whole-wheat flour, sugar, baking powder, cinnamon, and cloves.

Fold in carrot, zucchini, pineapple, sunflower seeds, and coconut.

Spoon batter into 6 greased muffin tins. Bake for 20 minutes. Makes 6 muffins.

Peach Almond Muffins

This is a great beginner muffin. Just add and mix.
A nice light and fresh flavor is your reward.

1¾ cups flour
½ cup sugar
1 tsp. baking powder
½ tsp. baking soda
½ cup sour cream
½ cup peaches, chopped, fresh
   or canned
1 egg
½ cup milk
1 tsp. almond extract
½ tsp. vanilla extract
½ cup sliced almonds

Preheat oven to 400°F. Mix all ingredients together except sliced almonds—do not over mix. Divide into 10 greased muffin tins. Sprinkle almond slices on top. Bake for 20 minutes.

Sweet Breads

Sweet Breads

The ultimate favorite of all breakfast foods.

● Sweet Bread Tips

Do not use spreads to replace real butter. Spreads contain less fat and more water, so they will not perform like butter or margarine. Margarine and shortening can be substituted for each other or for butter in almost any recipe.

Don't crowd the oven. Pans should never touch each other or the sides of the oven. Pans should also never be placed over or under each other on the racks.

Before preparing sweet bread dough, remove all of the ingredients from the refrigerator and let them sit on the counter for about an hour. Ingredients should be room temperature before use.

Check expiration date on all yeast packages. Yeast must be fresh to make the bread rise properly.

Cinnamon prevents yeast from properly rising bread. Thus, cinnamon is never mixed directly into yeast enhanced dough. Be careful not to contaminate measuring utensils with cinnamon. Designating specific measuring utensils to yeast and cinnamon can prevent contamination.

Cranberry Orange Scones

Jump start your morning with these delightful moist scones. In a pinch, raisins may be substituted. My personal favorite!

Scones:

2 cups flour
3 Tbsp. brown sugar
½ tsp. baking soda
½ tsp. salt
2 tsp. baking powder
½ tsp. vanilla
¼ cup butter
½ cup dried cranberries
1 tsp. orange peel, finely shredded
1 egg yolk, beaten
1 cup sour cream (8 oz. carton)

Orange Glaze:

1 cup powdered sugar, sifted
1 Tbsp. orange juice
¼ tsp. vanilla

Scones: In large mixing bowl combine flour, brown sugar, baking soda, salt, baking powder, and vanilla. Using a pastry blender or fork, cut in butter until mixture resembles coarse crumbs. Add dried cranberries and orange peel; toss to coat. Make a well in the center; set aside.

In small mixing bowl, combine egg yolk and sour cream—do not over mix. Pour egg mixture into well of dry mixture. Using a fork, stir all until combined (mixture may seem dry).

Turn dough out onto lightly floured surface. Quickly knead dough with 10 to 12 strokes or until almost smooth. Pat and roll dough into a 7-inch circle leaving the center of the circle thicker. Cut into 12 wedges.

Glaze: In small mixing bowl, stir together powdered sugar, orange juice, and vanilla. Stir in additional orange juice, 1 teaspoon at a time, until desired drizzling consistency is reached.

On an ungreased baking sheet, arrange wedges 1 inch apart. Heat oven to 400°F. Bake for 10 to 12 minutes or until golden brown. Cool on a wire rack for 10 minutes.

Drizzle glaze over top of scones. Serve warm. Makes 12 scones.

Cinnamon Buns from Heaven

With a whipped frosting to die for, it's no wonder these buns are from Heaven!

Dough:

2 pkgs. active dry yeast

1 cup warm water

2/3 cup plus 1 tsp. sugar, divided

1 cup warmed milk

2/3 cup butter

2 tsp. salt

2 eggs, slightly beaten

7–8 cups flour, more if needed

Filling:

1 cup melted butter, divided

1¾ cup sugar, divided

3 Tbsp. cinnamon

1½ cup chopped walnuts
 (optional)

1½ cup raisins (optional)

Frosting:

1 lb. margarine

1 lb. cream cheese

2 lbs. powdered sugar

2 tsp. vanilla extract

Dough: In small bowl, mix together warm water, yeast, and 1 teaspoon sugar; set aside. In large bowl, mix milk, remaining 2/3 cup sugar, melted butter, salt, and eggs; stir well and add yeast mixture. Add half the flour and beat until smooth. Stir in remaining flour until dough is slightly stiff (dough will be sticky).

Turn out onto a well-floured board; knead 5 to 10 minutes. Place in well-buttered glass or plastic bowl; cover and let rise in warm place until doubled in size, about 1 to 2 hours.

Roll out on a well floured board.

Filling: Spread dough with ½ cup melted butter. Mix together 1½ cups sugar and cinnamon; sprinkle over buttered dough. Sprinkle with walnuts and raisins, if desired.

Roll up jellyroll-fashion and pinch edge together to seal. Cut into 12 to 15 slices. Coat bottom of a 13x9-inch baking pan and an 8-inch square pan with remaining ½ cup melted butter. Then sprinkle with remaining ¼ cup sugar. Place cinnamon roll slices close together in pans. Cover; let

rise in warm place until dough is doubled in size, about 1 hour.

Heat oven to 350°F. Bake 25 to 30 minutes or until rolls are nicely browned. Cool rolls slightly.

Frosting: Allow margarine and cream cheese to reach room temperature. Beat cream cheese and margarine together in a bowl with a mixer. Slowly add in all powdered sugar. Once all sugar is in the bowl, mix for at least an additional 12 minutes. When almost done, add in the vanilla.

Chocolate Chip Caramel Rolls

Got milk? You'll need lots of it. You might want to double this recipe—one may not be enough!
It's okay, they're made in the microwave so they are fast and easy.

Caramel Mixture:

¼ cup brown sugar

1 Tbsp. corn syrup

2 Tbsp. margarine

Dough:

1 cup flour

1 Tbsp. wheat germ

1½ tsp. baking powder

3 Tbsp. shortening

¼ cup milk

1 Tbsp. margarine, melted

2 Tbsp. grated orange peel

¼ cup miniature semisweet
    chocolate chips

Caramel Mixture: In small bowl, combine brown sugar, corn syrup, and margarine. Cook on high for 1 to 2 minutes or until margarine is melted and brown sugar is dissolved. Stir to combine. Evenly divide mixture among 6 custard cups; set aside.

In large bowl, stir together flour, wheat germ, and baking powder. Cut in shortening till mixture resembles coarse crumbs. Add milk all at once; stir just until dough clings together. Turn onto a lightly floured surface. Knead gently 10 to 15 strokes. Roll flat into a rectangle. Pour melted margarine on dough and spread evenly. Sprinkle orange peel and chocolate chips over dough. Roll up jelly-roll style, beginning from short side. Seal seams.

Slice into 1-inch pieces. Place dough slices in custard cups, seam-side down. Arrange cups in a circle in the microwave oven. Cook on high for 2 to 3 minutes or till a toothpick comes out clean, turning and rearranging cups once after 1 minute. Let cool 1 minute. Loosen sides and invert onto a serving plate. Spread any remaining caramel mixture from cups onto rolls. Serve warm. Makes 6 rolls.

Carlene's Favorite Basic Dough Recipe

These cinnamon rolls are so easy! Bread machines are the greatest invention for the modern cook. Just add your ingredients and let it do all the work. Let the rolls rise in the refrigerator overnight so you can sleep in, and your family will think you're wonderful. This basic recipe is priceless.

Dough:
1½ cups water
2 Tbsp. sugar
2 Tbsp. olive oil
1¾ tsp. salt
4 cups flour
2 Tbsp. powdered milk
2½ tsp. yeast

Filling:
¼ cup butter
¼ cup sugar
½ cup brown sugar
4 Tbsp. cinnamon

Icing:
1 cup powdered sugar
2 Tbsp. milk
1 Tbsp. butter
¼ tsp. vanilla or almond extract

Dough: Place ingredients in bread machine in order as listed. Use dough setting.

When dough has finished mixing, roll dough onto a lightly floured board into a 10x12-inch rectangle.

Brush with butter; then sprinkle with sugar, brown sugar, and cinnamon.

Roll dough into a long tube. Cut into 15 equal pieces. Place slices in a 9x13-inch lightly greased pan. Cover rolls with sprayed plastic wrap. Let rise until double in size. These can be made the evening before and let rise during the night in the refrigerator.

Preheat oven to 350°F. Remove wrap; bake 15 to 20 minutes.

Icing: To make icing, follow Buttercream Icing instructions (see page 132). Ice while still warm.

Gooey Caramel Pecan Rolls

If you like caramel and pecans, this one is for you. These gooey rolls are wonderful.
Make sure you have lots of napkins on hand.

Carlene's Basic Dough Recipe
¾ cup brown sugar
½ cup heavy whipping cream
¼ cup chopped pecans

Make Carlene's Basic Dough Recipe (see page 121).

In sauce pan, combine brown sugar and heavy cream; heat and stir until sugar dissolves.

Grease a 9x13-inch baking pan. Sprinkle chopped pecans into bottom of pan.

Pour sugar mixture over pecans, spread evenly. Form bread dough into golf-ball size dough balls. Place dough balls onto pecans and sugar mixture. Cover with plastic wrap sprayed with non-stick spray.

Let rolls rise until double in size. Heat oven to 350°F. Bake for 15 to 20 minutes until lightly brown. Remove immediately from oven and invert onto a serving plate.

Fried Scones

My husband introduced me to these. His mother used to make them. My children love to use lots of butter, sprinkled with cinnamon and sugar. I like raspberry jam, honey, and powdered sugar. One of each, of course!

Carlene's Basic Dough Recipe
vegetable oil
toppings as desired

Make Carlene's Basic Dough Recipe (see page 121).

Heat vegetable oil 3 to 4 inches deep in pan, on medium high or 375°F. Take small amounts of dough and flatten each piece into a small 4- to 5-inch round circle. Fry dough on each side until golden brown. Remove from oil with tongs and drain on paper towels.

While still hot, serve with a variety of toppings such as butter, powdered sugar, honey, jam, or cinnamon and sugar.

Lemon Almond Pull-Aparts

Need an idea for a light brunch? This lemon and almond breakfast pull-apart is perfect.

Carlene's Basic Dough Recipe
½ cup sugar
2 lemon rinds, grated
¼ cup butter or margarine,
    melted
½ cup slivered almonds

Citrus Glaze:
1 Tbsp. butter, melted
1 cup powdered sugar
2 Tbsp. lemon juice

Make Carlene's Basic Dough Recipe (see page 121).

Mix sugar and lemon rind. Save ½ of mixture for just before baking. With scissors, cut dough into small pieces and roll into small balls. Place dough balls in a 9x13-inch greased baking pan. Pour butter over rolls. Cover with sprayed plastic wrap to let rise.

Let rise until double in size. Sprinkle remaining sugar-lemon mixture over dough. Preheat oven to 350°F. Remove wrap and bake 20 to 25 minutes. Remove from pan and cool on cooling rack.

Glaze: Combine butter, powdered sugar, and lemon juice. Mix well. Drizzle glaze over top. Sprinkle with slivered almonds. Serve warm.

Cinnamon Knots

These cinnamon knots are my daughter Sierra's favorite. If you like, make a double batch and you can try the orange version as well.

Carlene's Basic Dough Recipe
1 tsp. cinnamon
½ cup sugar
¼ cup butter, melted

Icing:
1 cup powdered sugar
1 Tbsp. butter, melted
2–3 Tbsp. milk
1 tsp. vanilla

Make Carlene's Basic Dough Recipe (see page 121).

Mix cinnamon with sugar. Cut dough into 18 pieces. Roll each piece into an 8-inch rope. Roll each knot in melted butter. Then roll into the cinnamon-sugar mixture. Tie the dough rope into a loose knot.

Grease 2 muffin pans. Place a knot in each hole. Cover with plastic wrap and let double in size.

Remove wrap. Bake at 350°F for 15 to 20 minutes or until golden brown. Remove from pan and place on a cooling rack. Brush with icing while still warm.

Icing: Cream powdered sugar and butter with an electric mixer. Add vanilla. Gradually add powdered sugar, scraping sides and bottom of bowl. Add milk and beat until light and fluffy.

Tip: To make Orange Rolls, just substitute 1 medium grated orange rind, for the cinnamon and 3 tablespoons orange juice for the milk. Use icing recipe. Bake as directed.

Toppings
and Glazes

Toppings and Glazes

Dress up any crumb cake or quick bread by giving it a powdered sugar glaze—it gives them a professional look.

● Topping and Glaze Tips

Before adding a glaze, make sure the cake or bread has cooled slightly; otherwise the glaze will merely be absorbed into the cake or bread.

A sieve or flour duster can be used to dust the surface when using powdered ingredients such as powdered sugar.

Some toppings and glazes are cooked, such as meringue-based frostings and chocolate glazes. Others, such as buttercream frostings, are often simply mixed together without having to do any cooking on the stove.

For a richer flavor, use real butter instead of shortening or margarine.

You can make a buttercream frosting ahead of time and keep it fresh in the refrigerator. To soften, just let it sit at room temperature. When the frosting softens, beat it with an electric mixer.

Quick Warm Blueberry Sauce

This will remind you of eating blueberries right off the bush.

....

2½ cups blueberries
⅓ cup sugar
½ cup orange juice
1 Tbsp. cornstarch
2 tsp. lemon juice

Combine blueberries, sugar, and ¼ cup orange juice in sauce pan. Warm mixture while stirring occasionally.

Blend cornstarch with remaining orange juice. Remove any lumps. Bring to a boil; add to sugar mixture.

Cook the sauce at a low boil for 1 minute, stirring constantly.

Remove the pan from heat and stir in lemon juice; will thicken as it cools.

Buttercream Icing

A nice, traditional icing for any topping.

½ cup solid shortening
½ cup butter
1 tsp. vanilla
4 cups powdered sugar
2 Tbsp. milk

Cream butter and shortening with electric mixer. Add vanilla. Gradually add powdered sugar, one cup at a time, beating well on medium speed. Scrape sides and bottom of bowl often.

When all sugar has been mixed in, icing will appear dry. Add milk and beat at medium speed until light and fluffy. Keep icing covered with a damp cloth until ready to use.

Tip: For best results, keep icing bowl in refrigerator when not in use. Rewhip before using.

Appleberry Sauce

A no-cook, no-fuss topper for pancakes, waffles, or French toast.
Substitute sugar-free jam if desired.

½ cup chunky unsweetened
    applesauce
¼ cup berry preserves
    (blackberry, blueberry, or
    strawberry)
1½ tsp. lemon juice

Combine all ingredients until smooth. To serve warm, heat fruit syrup in microwave on high for 30 minutes.

Oatmeal

Oatmeal

The oatmeal recipe that started it all.

5¼ cups water or milk
3 cups oats
¼ tsp. salt (optional)

On stove top boil water or milk and salt. Stir in oats. Cook about five minutes over medium heat; stir occasionally. Serve hot. Makes 6 servings.

Creamy Slow Cooker Oatmeal

This old-time favorite will save you some time in the morning by starting this oatmeal the evening before. It will be ready when you are. Quick and easy for all to enjoy.

4½ cups water
1½ cups oats
1½ cup half and half
1 tsp. vanilla
pinch of salt
½ cup brown sugar

Just before going to bed, combine the water and the oats in a slow cooker. Set to low, cover, and let cook overnight. In the morning, stir in the half-and-half, vanilla, and the salt. Scoop into bowls. Sprinkle with brown sugar. Makes 6 servings.

Triple Play Oatmeal

This creamy oatmeal is perfect with a nice cup of hot chocolate on those cozy winter mornings.

6 cups water
2 Tbsp. brown sugar
1 Tbsp. cinnamon
1 tsp. vanilla
$\frac{1}{3}$ cup maple syrup
3 cups uncooked rolled oats
$\frac{1}{2}$ cup raisins
3 medium apples, peeled,
   cored, and cubed

In large saucepan, combine water, brown sugar, cinnamon, vanilla, and maple syrup. Heat mixture to a boil. When water is at a boil, reduce heat and add in oats. Cook for about 5 minutes or until all water is soaked by the oats. Remove from heat; stir in apples and raisins. Makes 6 servings.

Chocolate Banana Oatmeal

The addition of chocolate in oatmeal makes it even more of a treat, and it is also a good way of enticing children to eat their oatmeal.

6 cups boiling water
3 cups rolled oats
¾ tsp. salt
1½ cups brown sugar
3 bananas, mashed
¾ cup semisweet chocolate
   morsels

In saucepan, combine water, oats, and salt. Simmer 5 minutes uncovered, stirring occasionally. Remove from heat and cover; let stand 3 minutes. Stir in brown sugar, bananas, and chocolate morsels. Serve with additional chocolate morsels sprinkled on top. Makes 6 servings.

Oven-Baked Oatmeal Topped with Raspberry Jam

If you do not want to stand at a stove to stir the oatmeal,
try this hands-off, oven-baked oatmeal.

1½ cup quick-cooking oatmeal
½ cup sugar
¼ cup butter, melted
½ cup milk
1 egg
¾ tsp. salt
1 tsp. baking powder
1½ tsp. vanilla
½ cup raspberry jam (set aside)

Preheat oven to 350°F. Grease a 13x9x2-inch baking pan.

Combine all ingredients together except raspberry jam. Spread into prepared baking pan. Drop spoonfuls of raspberry jam onto top of oatmeal—do not spread.

Bake for 25 to 30 minutes or until the edges are golden brown.

Spoon into bowls immediately. Top with warm milk.

Index

About the Author

Carlene Duda attended Ricks College (BYU–Idaho) and Brigham Young University. She is a culinary writer, teacher, and cook.

Her award-winning recipes have been published in newspapers and copyrighted by C&H Sugar Company. She is currently working on her next book.

Carlene Duda lives in Puyallup, Washington, with her husband, Scott, and their four children.

Photo by Brandy Stone